FREE PLANTS
FOR EVERYONE

Other Books by David the Good

Grow or Die: The Good Guide to Survival Gardening

Compost Everything: The Good Guide to Extreme Composting

Push the Zone: The Good Guide to Growing Tropical Plants Beyond the Tropics

Create Your Own Florida Food Forest

The Survival Gardener's Guide to Growing Your Own Caffeine

The Survival Gardener's Guide to Growing Your Own Tobacco

Turned Earth: A Jack Broccoli Novel

FREE PLANTS FOR EVERYONE

The Good Guide to Plant Propagation

David The Good

CASTALIA HOUSE

Free Plants for Everyone:
The Good Guide to Plant Propagation

David The Good

Published by Castalia House
Tampere, Finland
www.castaliahouse.com

Illustrations: David The Good
Cover: Andrew Chandler

Contents

Dedication

To my children, who regularly stick seeds and cuttings in pots all over the porch. Good work—and thank you for helping Mom while I was writing.

Introduction

I first discovered the power of seeds when I was in kindergarten. A teacher gave us beans and cups of soil in which to plant them. When a little bean plant unfurled its leaves a week later, I was hooked.

I'm not sure when I first learned about cuttings, but I do have a picture of my 12-year-old self and five of my siblings sitting behind a picnic bench by the road surrounded by plants I'd propagated, along with a big cardboard sign reading "plants".

At that point I'd already read extensively on grafting and cuttings, planted gardens for six years, plus wandered the neighborhood in search of interesting plants and seeds I could grow at home.

There's a magic to growing your own plants and bringing new life into the world. It's nowhere near as magical as the birth of a child, but there is a little fragment of that joy when you see a baby peach tree raise its head from the ground or a cluster of roots forming at the base of a frangipani cutting.

This book isn't a Deep And Very Serious Reference Work on Plant Propagation or a Definitive Guide to Seed-Saving. Instead, it's a rollicking jump right into growing and propagating everything from apples to zinnias, coffee to mesquite, and peaches to key limes.

As the father of eight children with another on the way, I know a lot about propagation—and about the need for frugality. I also know a lot about plants and have worked in the nursery business, running a small but profitable backyard nursery as well as working with a larger operation part-time.

Growing your own trees, shrubs, vines, vegetables and flowers is a lot cheaper than buying them from a nursery. So cheap it's often free. All you need is propagative material, whether that be roots, scions, seeds, cuttings or even aerial bulbils, as is the case with many of my beloved *Dioscorea* species.

Gardeners are the best people on the planet (after people with large families, of course) and most of them love sharing their plants with others. When I was a kid I scrounged seeds and cuttings from everywhere, but my best source was older ladies in the neighborhood. They were happy to share cuttings and tips on how to grow what they grew. All I needed to do was ask.

If there is a dark side to gardeners, however, it's their lust for plants. Though many are happy to share, they're usually not above pinching some seeds off a neighbor's cosmos or surreptitiously snipping a piece of variegated ivy off the arbor at a museum. And the lure of a botanical garden is often way too much for their green-thumbed greed. One gardening friend related sheepishly that he'd once stuffed a startling amount of cuttings into the base of his daughter's stroller while taking her to EPCOT.

It's easy to justify, of course. I've done it myself, much to my shame. It's easy to lose your morality when you picture yourself as the plant in the garden. It's practically begging to be taken!

"Oh please, someone! Help me reproduce! Please, kind sir, take my children to a new home!"

Meanwhile, you're trespassing in Mr. MacGregor's garden, which is bad because one day you'll get caught and made into a pie. It's much better to ask permission and be denied than it is to be a thief. Unless a plant is growing into the path or something. Or if some seeds just sort of fall into your hat. I have to repeat the eighth commandment to myself every time I walk through a botanical garden.

Truly, most plants are there for the asking. I have traded an abundance of wonderful plants with friends, some of whom I made by trading plants. Ask that old guy next door if you can have a cutting or two from his fig tree. See if the Indians at the gas station will share some seeds from their gardens. Ask the woman at work for some seeds from her Confederate rose. And be sure to bring cuttings and seeds of your own to share. It's great fun. The only downside is that your plant collection may grow too fast for you to manage. Do I hear a tiny violin?

If a gardener skipped the hunt for free seeds and cuttings and instead bought his plant collection from a nursery, he could spend thousands. When I grew my food forest in North Florida, most of my money was dropped on the first round of grafted fruit and nut trees. Though I could have grown my own, it would have taken more time than I wished to spend, so I traded money for time. With many of the other species, however, I propagated my own. I planted canna and arrowroot, ginger and yams, lilies and sunflowers, perennial African basil and nitrogen-fixers—an abundance of easy-to-propagate species for pollinators and food, beauty and medicine. Thousands of dollars retail for nothing but a little time and care.

Many times I would spend a little money for a plant I couldn't get for free, then I'd propagate the heck out of it. Thornless blackberries, for instance. Once you plant one, just bury the ends of the canes and the tips root into new plants. I grew a whole 15' x 15' patch of them this way, all from one original plant I bought for $10. If I'd bought them all, I would have spent $200—but there's no need when you know how to propagate. And I could have eventually grown $2,000 or even $20,000 worth of blackberry plants all from that one mother specimen.

What if instead of buying 30 shrubs for a hedge, you buy one shrub and start 40 cuttings from it? Accounting for failures and giveaways, you could plant your hedge for the cost of one plant. Get your cuttings from a neighbor and you may spend nothing.

It doesn't make sense with all plants, of course. Some trees and shrubs are slow to grow or a pain in the neck to propagate.

Hollies are usually too slow for my taste and too much of a pain to start from cuttings. Apple trees might make sense to buy, even though I love growing them from seed. Growing a live oak from an acorn may be too much of a time investment for you.

But once you get your first round of slowpokes purchased and growing, you can play around with acorns and apple seeds, and I encourage you to do so. Many of us have lost our ability to think generationally, and there's something transcendent in growing a tree you may never see mature.

Forget the philosophical angle for now, though, as it's beyond the scope of this book. You're probably reading this book because you want to know how to get lots and lots of plants for free—and I'm here to tell you it's easy as pie. I have a few hundred dollars worth of rare and exotic plants which I started just over the last year. Noni trees and coffee, mangoes and cocoa, purple yams and vanilla orchids. You can do the same with the plants around your neck of the woods and after reading this book you'll be raring to go.

Plants don't have to break the budget. In fact, they can even ease your budget. In the following chapters you'll learn how plants are propagated inside professional nurseries and how you can apply these methods in your own backyard. You'll also learn how to save seeds and grow things you've never been able to grow before. You'll learn how to mimic the timing of nature to get tricky seeds to sprout. You'll also lose your fear of grafting and start making solid grafts with materials you can scrounge at home.

Are you ready to make yourself a million bucks in free plants? Let's propagate!

1

10 Reasons to Propagate Your Own Plants

1. Your plants are FREE

Get a hibiscus cutting from a friend or snag an avocado pit and you can start a plant without spending a dime. If you grow something edible, you'll get free produce as well.

2. You can make some extra cash

I learned the basics of plant propagation as a kid and had my own little nursery business at age 11. You can too. Plenty of people will buy plants, even if you just put a few potted specimens out at your next garage sale. I actually wrote a little book on starting a plant nursery which bears the short and snappy title *The Easy Way to Start Your Own Home-Based Plant Nursery and Make Thousands in Your Spare Time*. Lots of people want to buy plants—if you are propagating, you can put some cash in your pocket.

3. Grow varieties no one has grown before

If you plant a fruit tree seed, you get a variety which is different from the parent tree. If Susan the Good Gardener plants a seed from a Gala apple, the tree that grows won't be exactly a Gala—it will be something new, due to the wonder of DNA. Susan can then name the variety after herself. Hey, it worked for Granny Smith.

4. You can make new friends

Nothing says "we are friends" like the gift of a plant. Except maybe the gift of a pizza. But most plants won't make you fat, so there is that. I am always propagating fruit and vegetable varieties and giving them away to friends and neighbors. If you start extra, you always have something to share when you're spontaneously invited to a dance party:

"Hey! I brought you a hibiscus!"

"WHAT? I TOTALLY CAN'T HEAR YOU OVER THE MUSIC! WHY DO YOU HAVE A PLANT."

"IT'S FOR YOU!"

"CAN YOU SMOKE IT?"

"NO, IT ISN'T CHOCOLATE!"

A friendship is born!

5. Personal satisfaction

When you eat sweet plums from a wild plum tree you tacked a graft onto a couple of years back, they taste better than anything else because you did it yourself. There are few things more satisfying than growing something healthy that you helped bring to life. It's a miracle.

6. You are helping plants

Plants want to reproduce, but mean, mean humans keep trimming them back, removing seed heads, packing them into landscape borders and defeating their primary desire in life. When you help them out by taking cuttings and planting their seeds, you become a friend to the plant world.

7. Did I mention your plants are free?

Think about how much money you'll save by propagating plants instead of buying them. My plant collection budget would run into the millions if I didn't know how to propagate.

8. You can save old varieties

Is there an old pear tree in your Grandma's yard that you remember as a child? Go find it and take a few little branches in the spring, then graft them onto some pear seedlings. Voila—you've saved the variety and will soon have Grandma's pear tree producing in your own yard.

9. You can improve your community

Are there very few pawpaw trees in your neighborhood? Find a good fruiting tree and plant the seeds, then share the potted seedlings with all your neighbors. See if the local park will let you plant a few. When you start plants from seeds, it costs nothing, so you can spread the trees all over the place.

10. You can guerrilla garden

When you have a bunch of seeds or some scion wood, you can go a step further than improving things by above-ground channels. You can grow plants wherever you like, in parks, empty lots, the yards of foreclosures, etc. Some enterprising gardeners have grafted fruiting pear wood onto ornamental pear varieties growing on public land. A few years later, those trees are bearing pears that local children and the homeless can pick and enjoy. Others have made "seed bombs" with wildflower mixes and tossed them into urban waste areas, carpeting trashy lots with beautiful blooms. It costs little to nothing, and it is much less likely to get you in trouble than spray-painting trains.

Alright! Are you stoked? Let's jump into how you can start growing zillions of free plants.

2

The Wild World of Seeds

Seeds are magic. Seeds are little stasis pods containing all the DNA required to create a tiny wildflower or a massive tree. Some seeds float on through the air on silken parachutes. Others float through the water to distant shores. Many are distributed in the dung of land animals or the droppings of birds. Some are ejected at high velocity like machine gun bullets or from pods which explode like hand grenades on hot days. Others hitch rides on the fur of passing animals or even on your socks.

When I was a child I watched a wonderful documentary created by Moody Science Films called *Journey of Life*, which fueled my excitement over seeds. As I've learned more, my fascination has only increased.

Before we get to the practical side of growing plants from seeds, let's take a journey into the wild world of seeds.

The Soil Seed Bank

A man once helped me take down some dangerous water oak trees in my backyard. While doing so, he drove through the wet grass in his pickup truck and left a few ruts in the ground. Those ruts opened my eyes to a whole new world. The rest of the yard was a mix of grasses with a few weeds here and there—yet in the bare soil ripped up by the pickup, a thick carpet of tiny sprouts appeared. And they weren't grass sprouts. They were a little, three-leafed sprout I first thought to be clover, but on further growth, proved to be black medic (*Medicago lupulina*), a nitrogen-fixing "weed".

According to the Purdue Extension:

> *Black Medic (*Medicago lupulina*) is a summer annual (or less commonly a winter annual) broadleaf weed that can be found throughout the United States. Seeds germinate in the spring and are capable of establishing in drought-prone or disturbed soils. Black medic is a legume, meaning that it has the capabilities to fix its own nitrogen; thus, allowing it to out compete turf in nutrient-poor soils as well.*[*]

Disturbed soils! Yes, that's exactly what I had in my backyard. Two ruts of disturbed soil filled with bright green black medic, surrounded by undisturbed grass.

---

[*] https://purdueturftips.blogspot.com/2014/04/weed-of-month-for-november-2013-is.html

How did it show up there? The answer: the soil seed bank.

Seeds are everywhere in the soil. They are scattered and buried, often laying dormant for years until proper conditions bring them to life. These conditions might be a flood, a fire, or a farmer's tractor. The seeds sleep in the soil until the time is right.

Construction sites are an excellent location to observe the power of the soil seed bank. Broken rock and dust and concrete and compacted soil abound, and yet in these harsh conditions, life appears. Pokeweed, pigweed, and fast-growing pioneer trees and plants pop up everywhere, in an attempt to repair the ecological damage. As I've written before, weeds are nature's Band-Aids. A construction site often has a completely different set of plants than you'll see growing right next door in an undisturbed area.

An abundance of nitrogen from animal manures triggers the growth of nettles. Compacted soil brings you thistles. And pickup truck ruts, I now know, get you patches of black medic.

These weeds grow, slowly bringing the ground back into balance, slowing or stopping erosion, fixing nitrogen, recreating humus, breaking up hard ground—it's an amazingly designed system, much like our body's wound-healing mechanisms.

Every time you dig the soil, more weeds show up. No wonder it's a never-ending battle for gardeners.

Compost Pile Bandits

We are regularly assured by composting experts that hot composting destroys seeds, yet I have harvested plenty of pumpkins which beg to differ.

Granted, most of my compost piles aren't regularly turned heaps, meaning that the seeds probably missed the hottest part of the compost—but how many of you turn your compost regularly yet still have little tomatoes and weeds pop up in it?

My bet is all of you.

Here's an example of "hot composting kills weed seeds" advice from Aggie Horticulture:

> *The composting process also naturally kills weed seeds. Properly managed, a compost pile should easily reach 140°F, which breaks down all organic matter, including weed seeds.* [*]

They recognize the difficulty, though, as the next line reads:

> *The key word is properly.*

My bet is that few gardeners reach that lofty, "proper" goal.

A typical backyard compost heap isn't insulated or turned often enough to maintain heat and rotate all the viable seeds in the compost through the hot center of the pile.

---

[*] http://aggie-horticulture.tamu.edu/vegetable/files/2010/10/E-326.-Easy-Gardening-Composting-to-Kill-Weed-Seeds.pdf

Yes, the heat generated by thermophilic bacteria in a hot compost pile is high enough to destroy seeds, but getting every bit of your compostable materials hot enough to kill the seeds takes very good compost management.

I imagine if you owned a cement truck and packed the barrel of it with a proper mix of carboniferous and nitrogenous materials, then rotated it every day or so, and perhaps insulated the inside with foam, you could get that compost to heat up perfectly.

I'm joking. A bit.

My composting methods have gone from complicated to simple over the years as I've realized creating perfect compost doesn't really matter.

Nature doesn't create perfectly sifted, totally rotted-down brown humus. No, she throws logs and leaves on the ground. There's always some finished material and some fresh material, some fungi eating at this and some insect boring away at that.

I always get volunteer tomatoes, wheat from straw, weeds, and pumpkins popping up even from hot piles. Knowing this, it takes a lot of faith in your compost-fu to deliberately throw in weedy materials.

If you have spiny pigweed going to seed in your food forest, do you really want to throw that in your compost bin and then use the resulting compost in your spring gardens?

Not I. I can't even keep pumpkins from becoming invasive.

Though you might be able to work out your systems so all seeds are destroyed, it's not really necessary.

In *Compost Everything* and on my YouTube channel, I share one of my favorite composting methods, where I simply designate a garden bed as my compost pile and dump all the kitchen scraps and garden waste there for six months or so and let it rot down. This forms compost and feeds the ground where I'll soon plant future crops. When I did this on a tropical farm we rented, tons of tropical fruit trees sprouted in the pile. I got mangoes, avocados, papaya, Malay apples and even cocoa. This was a feature, not a bug, as I simply potted up lots of these volunteers for future planting. When you eat a lot of vegetables, you can often just let compost piles turn into garden beds in the spring since there are so many volunteer edibles coming up from the feasts of yesteryear.

Instead of composting in my garden compost piles, back on my North Florida homestead I would just chop down weeds and throw them on the ground around my fruit trees and other shrubs. There they will return to the soil without popping up in your petunias.

Unlike delicate annual garden plants such as lettuce and cabbage, trees and shrubs don't need to be perfectly weeded in order to produce. I just knocked down the weeds again and again, and every time I did, guess what?

Those fallen weeds rotted into humus.

Nature does this all the time. The winter freezes come once a year and toast all the weeds, letting them fall down and rot into the soil, improving it. The Bible instructed the children of Israel to let their land go completely fallow one year out of seven. Weeds regenerate the soil.

If you want to use weeds to feed your gardens, you'll have much better luck in a no-till system where you throw a pile of seedy weeds on the ground, then cover them up with mulch… and then DON'T TILL!

If you till, you'll bring those seeds up to the light and warmth and they'll go crazy in your eggplants. Beneath a layer of mulch, however, they'll eventually rot away safely.

You can also throw your weeds to the chickens and turn garden trouble into golden-yolked eggs.

That's my two cents on composting destroying seeds. Yes, it can be done—but most of us aren't doing it "properly", so don't trust too much in the magic of compost.

Personally, I prefer cold composting anyhow as I believe it keeps more of the good stuff in the pile instead of steaming away into the air. Nature almost always cold composts, and while that process takes longer I think it's a simpler and gentler method.

Seeds are magic, and weed seeds are black magic. Don't curse your compost if you can help it.

Seeds That Want to Be Eaten and Seeds That Don't

Some seeds want you to eat them. Tomato seeds, for instance. Others, like the deadly poisonous rosary pea (*Abrus precatorius*) obviously do not.

The fruits of plants are often designed to be delicious to animals and humans, ensuring that their seeds will be carried away and planted either by being spit somewhere or swallowed and eventually planted in a nice, fertile pat of manure. Monkeys, squirrels, bird and even bats excel at accidental planting. As a 1987 article in BATS Magazine reports:

> *The fruits of pioneer plants, those that are first to populate cleared areas of forest, contain enormous quantities of small seeds which are usually eaten by a diverse group of fruit-eating birds and mammals. Except for these, tropical plants appear to have specialized on particular groups of animals for dissemination of their seeds. For example, Charles Janson reported that two-thirds of the 258 species of fruit he examined in a Peruvian moist tropical forest could be classified as 'bird' or 'mammal' fruits. Bird fruits were characterized as being relatively small, unprotected by a husk, and either red, black, white, blue, or purple in color. In contrast, mammal fruits were characterized as being large, often protected by a husk, and either orange, yellow, brown, or green in color. Mammal fruits can be further subdivided into primate and bat fruits, with the latter often occurring in the plant*

families to which figs and their relatives belong (Moraceae),
the chicle family (Sapotaceae), myrtle (Myrtaceae), palm
(Palmae), black pepper (Piperaceae), and tomato families
(Solanaceae).

Two families of bats, the neotropical leaf or spear-nosed
bats (Phyllostomidae) and the paleotropical flying foxes
(Pteropodidae), each contain over 100 species of fruit-eaters
responsible for dispersing seeds from hundreds of species of
tropical trees and shrubs. Many of these bats also pollinate
a broad variety of plants, including a large number that are
commercially valuable. Bats of these two families are often
among the most numerous of all tropical mammals in undis-
turbed tropical forests, where they are unpersecuted by man.
By virtue of their abundance and highly mobile lifestyles, these
animals play an essential role in the seed dispersal ecology of
tropical forests.[*]

On the other end of the spectrum, there are seeds which
are highly toxic, such as the aforementioned rosary pea, or the
well-known super-toxic castor bean (*Ricinus communis*). Their
reproductive strategy is the "Leave me the heck alone, I'll sprout
without your help, thank you very much!" approach.

Often, the fruit of a plant is edible but the seeds are bitter or
poisonous or both. Many have seeds with both hard coats and

---

[*] http://www.batcon.org/resources/media-education/bats-magazine/bat_article/289?
tmpl=component

toxic interiors, such as the soursop or the peach. "You can eat the fruit," says the tree. "Just don't digest my baby!"

Many of our favorite vegetables and flowers grow easily from seeds. Simply prepare some soil and plant, then water, then a week or two later, you have seedlings. Sure, some are a little tricky, like beets with their multiple sprouts coming from one "seed"—which is actually a little fruit—or carrots, with their need to be near the surface and their pokey germination; but most of our garden plants are just "read the directions on the seed pack" simple.

Anyone can sprout beans or peppers, so I'm not going to share much on how to do that, except to cover why I prefer direct seeding to transplants.

Direct Seeding vs. Transplants

In cold climates with short growing seasons, growing transplants for the garden makes a lot of sense. Some plants just take too long to produce and if you don't get a head-start, you won't have much luck with your garden. However, sometimes that "head-start" isn't much of a head-start, because of transplant shock. Some plants—like peppers—barely care if they're transplanted. Others—like melons—really suffer from root disruption. I believe in direct seeding when you can. I've seen direct-seeded plants outpace transplants which were much bigger. If you've ever moved from one house to another, you know it's stressful. It's even worse for plants, even when you count in the fact that they're not hauling sleeper sofas and boxes of books. A seed planted directly in the ground can drive its roots deep. It never has to adjust to completely different soil conditions, or lose roots in a move, or suffer being root-bound. My primary reason for preferring direct seeding is that it's less stressful on the plants and gives them a better start in life.

That said, there is a second reason to prefer direct seeding— it's way cheaper! Compare the price of seeds to transplants and the difference is stark. A packet of fifty seeds is a buck or two. Fifty transplants is likely to run you about twenty times that price. Unless you're growing your own transplants because of a short growing season, direct seeding is preferable.

Vegetable gardens aside, direct seeding trees is also a great way to grow. I've direct seeded pawpaw, persimmon, nut trees and even jackfruit. Those trees delve deep right from infancy and are stronger than a transplanted container-grown tree.

Since seeds are cheap, I usually direct seed by planting multiple seeds, then later thinning with scissors, removing all but the best specimen. This works really well with papaya in the yard. It's also a very good way to grow a garden bed, especially when you're working with older seed or in tough conditions. A lot of seedlings may be lost at the beginning, though sometimes they aren't. When nature doesn't thin, you can. It's no sweat to over-plant a bit so long as seeds are cheap.

I do skip direct seeding sometimes, though. When I have a rare specimen, few seeds, or a species with slow or difficult germination, it may make sense to grow in pots, far from the cutworms.

Heirlooms, Hybrids and GMOs

In the realm of gardening, there are few topics more touchy than seeds. You'd think they'd be a safe area of conversation, but nope. Not anymore. Not since GMOs came along and scared the pants off people. Now when I mention growing corn, I often hear statements like "BUT CORN IS GMO!" or "BE CAREFUL!"

And it's not just corn. Heck, I've had people ask me questions about everything from herbs to roots. I understand the concern. I'm no fan of cutting and pasting genes cross-species. In fact, I think it's downright evil and against the natural order. No one in their right mind wants jellyfish genes in their potatoes. Yet a lot of the concern about GMOs goes far beyond the plants which are normally genetically modified. A gardener will tell you he only uses "heirloom" seeds as if heirloom varieties were a crucifix held at arm's length against an approaching vampire.

I love heirlooms; however, they're not the only seeds unaffected by genetic modification. Most seeds are not GMO. I would even venture to say most gardeners haven't yet encountered GMO seeds.

Yet a lot of people look sideways at the seed racks in the local store, assuming that the big vegetable seed companies must be selling GMOs to home gardeners. Fortunately, this isn't the case—at least not purposely.

George Ball, CEO of Burpee, was so tired of the rumors he posted a public statement on the Burpee website titled 'Burpee, GMO And Monsanto Rumors Put To Rest':

I and others at Burpee are asked occassionally [sic] about our alleged connection to Monsanto and whether we sell GMO seed. We have even been accused of being owned by Monsanto on the Internet. I've decided to address these questions and false allegations formally with the hopes that someone out there in cyberspace may refer back to this post for information on these issues—straight from the source.

For the record, I own W. Atlee Burpee & Co. Burpee is NOT owned by Monsanto. We do purchase a small number of seeds from the garden seed department of Seminis, a Monsanto subsidiary, and so do our biggest competitors. We do NOT sell GMO seed, never have in the past, and will not sell it in the future.

Another commonly seen seed company, Ferry-Morse (owned by Plantation Products), released this statement from their CEO:

[W]e have been around for a long time and do not sell GMO seeds in any of our product lines, nor does our company plan to do so in the future. We do not feel the need to copy a

few smaller seed companies by putting up signs on our retail
displays because it creates an impression that other seed compa-
nies are using GMO seeds. The truth of the matter is that no
seed company selling seed packets for $1–$2 to home gardeners
could ever afford seeds that have been genetically modified,
nor could I imagine that any legitimate seed company would
jeopardize their reputation by selling such GMO seeds to the
public.

Those who argue in favor of GMOs often claim that mankind
has been "genetically engineering" plants for thousands of years
by selecting and breeding for desired traits. This is a lousy,
lying and misrepresentative argument. There's a big difference
between breeding within a species and splicing in genes from
other species. Genetic modification creates crosses that are ab-
solutely impossible in nature. Breeding wild grasses into usable
grains or selecting for the biggest blackberry bushes in the patch
is natural. Putting bacteria genes into corn is not—but I'm
getting ahead of myself.

Let's take a quick look at what makes a seed an heirloom, a
hybrid or a GMO.

Heirloom Seeds

Heirloom seeds are open-pollinated seeds which have been
passed down generationally. At least, that's the general defini-
tion. Open-pollinated means the plant was pollinated naturally,

whether by bird of beast, wind or insect. Heirlooms, so long as they're not planted next to other plants of the same species (unless they're self-pollinators), will set seed and you'll get the same variety year after year. They've been "stabilized" to a point where the plants are a consistent type, yet there's always a little variation. This variation is to your advantage, however, as it allows the variety to adapt to your garden as you plant it year after year. If you save and plant Blue Hubbard squash seeds, they are going to give you Blue Hubbard squash. Save the seeds in the fall and you'll get the same variety again next year… and the next year… and the next. Heirlooms have been bred to a level of consistency over years of growing.

Hybrid Seeds

Hybrids, unlike heirlooms, are not open-pollinated. Instead, they are the result of a deliberate cross between two parents within the same species in order to create a single generation of vigorously growing crops with specific genetic expressions. If you plant a hybrid tomato variety, you should get great tomatoes that season. Yet, if you save the seeds, all bets are off. Hybrids are not GMO. They're more expensive than open-pollinated seeds because it takes extra effort to cross lines and produce the seed, but they don't cross the species barrier and there is no gene tinkering taking place. You can save the seeds from hybrids and often get a decent crop—but it's going to be a different variety than what you got the first year. I prefer to skip the hybrids and just grow heirlooms, but some gardeners like the exact and consistent results a hybrid can provide.

GMO Seeds

GMO seed is a whole different animal... er, plant. It's expensive to produce and takes high technology to pull off, so you're not going to be able to do it at home, no matter how much you wish you could add firefly genes to your favorite cherry tomato.

According to Harvard University:

> *Altering the genome of plant seeds is difficult due to their rigid structure. Many biotech companies use 'gene guns' that shoot metal particles coated with DNA into plant tissue with a .22-caliber charge. Monsanto no longer uses gene guns, but instead takes advantage of bacteria, called* Agrobacterium tumefaciens, *that naturally invade seeds and alter plants by inserting pieces of their own DNA into a plant's genome. ... After a genetic trait has been successfully inserted into an organism's genome, the modified organism must then be able to grow and replicate with its newly engineered genome. First, the genotype of the organisms must be checked so that researchers are only propagating organisms in which the genome was modified correctly. Biotech companies invest large sums into keeping these plants alive and reproducing once they have been successfully created. The companies use special climate-controlled growth chambers, and biologists often check on the*

plants by hand to make sure that they are growing as expected. During this process biotech companies will use automated machines, such as Monsanto's GenV planter, in order to track plants and calculate optimal seeding and growth conditions to create the best possible yields.[*]

Since the average person doesn't understand how this works, he will often assume that anything strange is GMO. Yellow watermelons, Cornish Cross chickens, extra large pumpkins, his mother-in-law, etc. That isn't the case. Genetic modification is a pain in the neck to pull off and you're not likely to come across GMO seeds for your garden. However, there is another GMO risk.

GMO Contamination of Crops

Some plants (I'm looking at you, corn) are very promiscuous, spreading their pollen to the winds with abandon. If you plant an heirloom corn such as Hickory King next to a field of GMO corn, they will cross and when you save seeds, you'll have some of that GMO DNA in your seed line. Over time, it may be impossible to unthread the needle and get back to traditional heirlooms, uncontaminated by genetic tinkering. Nassim Nicholas Taleb is one of my favorite authors and thinkers and his take on the risk of GMOs resonates with my own. He writes:

---

[*] http://sitn.hms.harvard.edu/flash/2015/how-to-make-a-gmo/

Ecologically, in addition to intentional cultivation, GMOs have the propensity to spread uncontrollably, and thus their risks cannot be localized. The cross-breeding of wild-type plants with genetically modified ones prevents their disentangling, leading to irreversible system-wide effects with unknown downsides. The ecological implications of releasing modified organisms into the wild are not tested empirically before release.

Healthwise, the modification of crops impacts everyone. Corn, one of the primary GMO crops, is not only eaten fresh or as cereals, but is also a major component of processed foods in the form of high-fructose corn syrup, corn oil, corn starch and corn meal. In 2014 in the US almost 90% of corn and 94% of soybeans are GMO.

Foods derived from GMOs are not tested in humans before they are marketed. The widespread impacts of GMOs on ecologies and human health imply they are in the domain of the PP (Precautionary Principle). This should itself compel policy makers to take extreme caution.[*]

I agree, and I could go on and on about GMOs, but that's not the point of this book. We need to get growing something, so let's quit worrying about the evils of science and start planting.

---

[*] http://nassimtaleb.org/tag/gmo/

3

Germinating Seeds Like a Boss

As we've learned from our quick look at the soil seed bank, some seeds only like to sprout under certain conditions. Generally, this is because they're optimized to sprout at a time optimal for growth. If a peach pit sprouted in fall, the young seedling would get killed by frost, so instead of instant germination, peaches and other stone fruit have built in timers that start ticking when cold sets in. Other seeds have hard coats that protect the embryo until conditions are right. Yet other seeds wait for sunshine to activate their germination. They may lie buried in your fescue until a plumber digs up a pipe and turns the soil, then they burst into life. And don't forget the seeds that like to pass through a digestive tract first, perhaps traveling miles by air in the belly of a bird before being bombed into your vegetable garden. Let's look at how to sprout these seeds first—with ACID!

Acid Treating Seeds

This is not a method I prefer—even though it sounds awesome—but it often gives excellent results. To do it, you need some strong acid—and you need to be careful. FAO gives a procedure:

> *Safety precautions require strict attention as concentrated sulphuric acid is dangerous to people and materials. It should be handled at all times with great care. When mixed with water it produces a violent exothermic reaction. Water should never be added to the acid or it may boil explosively. If a dilute mixture is required the acid must be allowed to trickle slowly into stirred water. All operators should wear acid-resistant protective clothing, gloves and eye protection. A solution of sodium or potassium bicarbonate should be kept readily available as an antidote to accidental skin contact with the acid (FAO 1974a).*

> *A procedure for acid scarification, based on Bonner et al. (1974), is as follows:*

> 1. *Allow seeds to come to air temperature and make sure the seed surface is dry.*

> 2. *Completely immerse the seeds in undiluted acid (1,200 ml per kg of seed) for the required period. The treatment is best carried out at 20°–*

> *27°C; lower temperatures require longer soak-*
> *ing times.*
>
> 3. *Remove the seeds from the acid, immediately*
>   *wash them thoroughly in cool running water*
>   *for 5–10 minutes to remove all traces of acid.*
>   *Use a large amount of water at the start of the*
>   *washing and stir carefully.*
>
> 4. *Spread the seeds in a thin layer for surface dry-*
>   *ing, unless wet sowing is preferred.*

The optimum soaking period will depend on the species. It is
usually in the range 20–60 minutes.[*]

Green Deane, creator of the popular plant foraging site
www.eattheweeds.com, shared with me that "pokeweed seeds
have a germination rate of about 6% until soaked in battery
acid. Then it's over 90%."

Acid treatment is useful for hard seeds and is common in
science labs, though you can usually skip it and use less scary
methods.

Boiling Water

Some trees and plants have seeds with hard coats. This allows a
seed to remain in the soil, sometimes for years, and then grow

---

[*] http://www.fao.org/docrep/006/Q2190E/Q2190E07.htm

when it's good and ready and the conditions are perfect. We gardeners don't have time for all that. We want a seed to pop up within a reasonable time frame. Boiling water can help.

I wouldn't use this method on tiny seeds as I think it's likely to kill them, but for bigger seeds such as *Leucaena* or tamarind or carob or winged bean, it shouldn't hurt.

Put some seeds in a container that can handle boiling water, then put a pot of water on the stove and bring it to a boil. Once it's boiling, take it off the stove and pour it into your container of seeds, then let the seeds sit for half a day or overnight. You'll see some or all of them swell and take on water, loosening their hard seed coats. Plant those. Some seeds may remain hard and you can pour boiling water on them again if you wish, then let them soak. The second or third time might be the charm.

Chitting

"Chitting" seeds means pre-sprouting them. If you've got an old pack of sunflower seeds and you're not sure how many will grow and don't want to spend time planting them all in a row just to end up with maybe one plant, chitting is your friend. It's also a good way to grow rare or expensive seeds and make sure you get every one going without entrusting them to the ground and the critters.

If you've ever grown your own sprouts at home, you've already chitted seeds. One method is to take a paper towel, dampen it and squeeze it out, then lay some seeds on one side and fold the other side over on the seeds. Then place the towel and its enclosed seeds in a plastic bad to retain moisture. In a few days, the seeds should start sprouting. When you see roots or shoots, plant them out.

Another method is to chit your seeds in a jar or other container. First, soak your seeds for a few hours, then strain them out of the water and put them in a container with a lid or a piece of cheesecloth over the top. A few times a day, rinse the seeds out and re-wet them. In a few days, they'll start sprouting and can be planted. The cheesecloth is nice because you can pour water into the jar through the cheesecloth, then swish the seeds around inside, then pour the water out again. I don't have any cheesecloth on hand, so I just swish the seeds in the bottom of a jar and strain with my fingers. If any fall into the drain, I save them and throw them back in.

Scarification

Scarification isn't some bloody ritual practice from the dark heart of Africa. Well, actually it is, but it's not when you're talking about seeds. Scarifying seeds is the act of abrading or cutting the seeds in some way to break the integrity of the seed coat and raise the germination rate. It works wonders on hard seeds—particularly those of leguminous species such as *Albizia spp.*, carob (*Ceratonia siliqua*), tamarind and hamburger bean (*Mucuna urens*). Canna seeds are another one that benefit from scarification, as do water lotus seeds (*Nelumbo nucifera* and *Nelumbo lutea*). This is my go-to method.

There are multiple ways to scarify seeds. You can use a pair of scissors, a pocketknife (careful!), nail clippers, rubbing the seed over sandpaper, or a file. Triangular files work great for cutting little notches into seeds.

If you know where the embryo in a seed is—with beans, for instance, it's around the dimple—don't cut there. Cut into the side or back, just enough to puncture the seed coat a little bit so water can get inside. After I scarify seeds, I soak them in water overnight, then plant them the next day. It's amazing how fast supposedly "hard to germinate" seeds will germinate if you break their seed coats. In nature, this might happen in the gut of an animal (there's a reason acid works) or thanks to freezing temperatures, or the eventual decay of the seed coat by the elements. Practically, scarification gives you really great results with tough seeds. If you've had hard luck germinating specific species with hard seed coats, consider nicking them, giving them a soak, and trying again. My bet is you'll be pleasantly surprised by your success. As I write this chapter, I have a Tupperware of dwarf pink banana (*Musa velutina*) plants on my porch, just starting to grow and reach for the light. They are known to take months to sprout—yet with scarification, I germinated their seeds three weeks after planting.

Stratification

This method is really awesome.

Did you know some seeds have little timers built into them that only go off after a period of cold, or heat, or both?

If you plant a peach pit in a pot, it won't germinate unless it gets some cold weather first. This is because peach pits are designed to hit the ground in summer, then be planted by the rains and the falling leaves, then go through the cold of winter. In winter, they'll start forming roots, and then when the weather warms up—*pop!*—up comes the shoot of a brand-new baby peach tree.

If peach pits sprouted when they first hit the ground, the young tree would emerge a short time before winter and its tender life would be lost to the frosts.

Once you realize how peach pits are designed, you can trigger their germination easily. Just get yourself a peach pit, put it in some slightly moist medium (vermiculite, potting soil, loose sand, or whatever), then put it in the fridge. Roots usually start to emerge from the pit in 2–3 months. When you see them popping out, you can plant the pit and it will grow into a tree. I started dozens this way and gave away lots of peach trees to friends.

The same method works for cherries, plums and other stone fruits, American persimmons, pawpaws (*Asimina spp.*), apples, pears, walnuts, strawberries, redbuds, pecans and many other temperate species. You can also plant many of these seeds in the ground in fall and let nature do it for you; however, sometimes nature also sends critters to eat your seeds, or you forget where you planted them.

If you're dealing with a temperate fruit or nut tree, chances are you'll have to stratify it in some way to get it to sprout.

Seeds that Shouldn't Dry Out

Clean 'em, dry 'em, and stick 'em in an envelope. That's the normal way to store seeds, but some seeds don't like storing. Particularly tropical seeds. They are often designed to hit the ground and start growing right away, unlike their temperate cousins. The window of viability on some species is vanishingly short, with tropical fruits like canistel, mango, jackfruit, citrus and others giving up the ghost within days or weeks if they aren't planted in the ground.

A woman once wrote me and said "I tried planting some lemon seeds but they never came up—what's the trick?" I asked how she had treated the seeds, and she said she had dried them thoroughly, then planted them.

Nope. They're dead. The embryo inside a lemon seed will die if it dries out all the way. With a lot of these tropical species, just pretend you're a fruit bat and eat the fruit, then plant the seed right afterwards. But don't plant it the way fruit bats do. That would be gross.

Light to Germinate

Some seeds are designed to germinate when they are near the surface of the soil. If they're too deep, they won't sprout. This is a novel innovation, as it means deeply buried seeds will "sleep" in the soil until there is a disruption that turns them up to the light, upon which they emerge to repair the damage done to the ground. In this category fall many tiny seeds, including lettuce, tomato, poppies and others. If you plant too deeply, they will never emerge. Tobacco is one of these. The way I've started seeds like this is to sprinkle them on the surface of some moist soil in a flat, then very lightly stir them in with my fingertips, or just pat them into the soil, then cover the flat with some plastic wrap to let in the light but keep the moisture from leaving. If these tiny seeds sprout and then the sun dries them out, they're toast. It's important that they get a chance to get their roots down into the ground before they face moisture stress. Once they grow to be a couple of inches tall, transplant them to their final home.

Learn your species and try these methods accordingly and you'll be able to sprout just about any seed.

Now let's look at cuttings.

4

Redneck Rooting

Plant nurseries use strange and often complex systems to vegetatively propagate plants. I have visited a few large commercial nurseries which used cloning to grow a wide variety of beautiful plants. That is way beyond my skill set, not to mention my budget.

Closer to my budget are the misting systems and rooting hormones used to start tray after tray of plants at smaller nurseries. I built a backyard mist house once and will share with you how to do the same, but it's not for everyone. I wouldn't have done it if I weren't making money, and it's too much trouble for most of us. Let's look at some easier ways.

The Mini-Greenhouse Method

My go-to method of rooting cuttings is the mini-greenhouse method. All you need is a baggie, a container, some soil, a rubber band and a cutting you'd like to root.

Good cuttings are important. If you take cuttings from an weak, over-fertilized or pest-infected mother plant, they're less likely to do well. It's also important to take cuttings from branches that aren't too soft. New growth often rots when you try to root it. Old growth is sometimes reticent to make roots and will do nothing. I usually shoot for something in between, going for a bit older wood which is still moderately recent growth. Don't worry, though, if all this sounds confusing. Just take cuttings from all over the place and try them. The best way to learn what works and what doesn't is to DO IT! If you're not sure if a plant will root from cuttings or not, don't fret over it. Just try it and see, then you'll know for the future. A few minutes of experimentation can be worth an hour of research online.

On most plants I go for 4–6" cuttings with at least two nodes. Nodes are the growing points where leaves emerge. One will be buried to produce roots, the other will produce new leaves and vines. Some plants root right from the nodes, others don't. If you don't know, there's no harm in burying a node. When you take your cuttings, use something sharp. I have some good Felco hand pruning shears I like to use. It's not good to mash the stems—sharp, clean cuts are important. Just don't cut your own fingers off, unless you plan to clone yourself.

Now fill a small container with loose, moist soil.

I've used plastic nursery pots, old tomato sauce cans, water bottles with the tops cut off, yogurt cups, plastic bags, nursery pots or whatever else happens to be around. Plants don't have eyes and are incapable of embarrassment, so they don't care much where they're planted.

Now it's time to stick your cuttings.

Cuttings can be damaged and may rot if you simply cram them into the ground. It's better to punch a little hole, then pop them in. I usually use a stick as a dibbler.

Some plants root very easily so I don't bother using rooting hormone on them. Generally, though, it's a good idea to dip your cuttings in rooting hormone before planting. You can get rooting hormone powder in the garden section of almost any home improvement store.

Pop your cuttings in the hole made by your piece of stick, then firm the dirt around their stems.

Now it's time to start making a mini greenhouse. Take a stick and put it in the middle of the soil next to your cutting, pressing it in so it's firmly upright. Now put a clear plastic bag over the stick.

Now rubber-band that bag into place, and voila—you have your mini-greenhouse.

White grocery bags will also work, though you can't see your cuttings as easily.

Once you've bagged up these pots, place them in the shade. If they're in the sun, they'll cook.

Open them up every few days to let a little air in. I like to blow into the bags to give them some extra carbon dioxide, but that's just me.

Coleus rooting in a mini greenhouse

After a few weeks, your cuttings should start rooting. When they're firmly rooted, remove the bags and plant them up in pots of their own. Just a little tug on the stem will tell you if the roots have caught.

Rooting cuttings the easy way takes a few minutes and cheap materials.

An alternate method that has worked for me is to get a basin and put a little water in the bottom of it—say an inch or two—then put my cuttings in pots sitting in that water. Once all the cuttings are done, I put a white trash bag over the entire bin and tie it shut to keep in the moisture, then I ignore it for a month or two someplace in the shade. When I come back, my cuttings are rooted. It's really easy.

The most important thing is to remember that your cuttings will die if they dry out. Without roots, they are very vulnerable.

Once your cuttings have decent root development, carefully prise them out of their pots and plant them while taking care not to disturb their young roots.

Try it at home—you'll be impressed by how well it works.

It's not rocket science. I once stuck some acerola cherry cuttings into some tin cans of soil, watered them, then tied them up in white plastic grocery bags, then forgot about them a few months. Literally. I had stuck them half-under the potting bench. Out of sight, out of mind. When I found them again, I couldn't remember what was in the bags, so I opened them up and discovered most of my cuttings had rooted and looked great. One of them is growing on my porch in a big pot right now.

The key is keeping them moist but not totally soaked. If they're swampy, they'll rot. If they're moist, they'll grow. If they're dry, they'll fail. Just use something to keep a humid atmosphere around the cuttings. If you're the DIY sort, you can make a little propagation cabinet or even an entire greenhouse to start cuttings. Or you can just use plastic bags or even one of those clear plastic clamshell cake containers from the local bakery. Just keep the humidity up and you'll have much more success than if you just stick cuttings and water them. With the mini-greenhouse method I rarely even have to water the cuttings after sticking them. The bag is enough to keep in moisture during the rooting period.

The "Jamming Things in the Ground" Method

Some plants are capable of rooting from a branch jammed in the ground. Some people have told me they stuck mulberry branches in the ground and had them root. Green Deane reports the same on his site, writing:

> *One spring I trimmed my mulberry and used the branches for stakes. They rooted and grew. Not one to get in nature's way I dug them up, gave them to a friend, and they are still growing.*[*]

---

[*] http://www.eattheweeds.com/mulberry-glucose-controlling-hallucinogen-2/

I didn't have that luck with mulberries, but it works great for a certain limited set of plants, including willow, *Gliricidia sepium*, frangipani, cassava, Mexican tree spinach, *Aralia spp.*, gumbo limbo, katuk, and others.

Most plants don't do well with this method, however, so don't rely on it for everything. No harm in trying, though.

I don't really recommend "jamming" them in the ground, though. It's better to punch a hole, then put in the plant. If you smash up the bottom of the stem too much it may just rot.

Something I have found interesting since moving to the tropics is how much better plants will root here in clay during the rainy season. Back in Florida I had sandy soil, which was easy to stick cuttings into; however, they would often dry out and die. Here, the ground is usually clay, but if you punch a hole in it and plant a branch, quite a few things will root. Locals even tell me that you can ram a branch of a calabash tree into the ground and it will root, even though that isn't a recommended method anywhere I've read.

If you have soil that holds water well, you may have better luck with taking stick cuttings and putting them in the ground. Willow is well-known for growing into a living fence when branches are planted. The branches can be interwoven at planting for a stunning effect, like living latticework. When I was a kid, my dad and grandpa always had aralia hedges. The variety of aralia they had possessed a very vertical growth habit and would grow a cluster of shoots that went almost straight up. To plant a new fence, dad and grandpa would cut some stems at 4–6′ in length and plant them in a row a foot apart, burying about a foot or so of the bottom of the stem in the ground. Then they'd water the cuttings in and wait. A few months later, all of them would be rooted and growing.

Over the next year, the fence would fill in and create a beautiful screen of green.

A couple of years ago I did something similar with *Gliricidia sepium* branches, except I got a little more creative with my planting, planting at a 45-degree angle and crossing and tying the branches as I went to make a lattice like the willow ones I had seen in photos. There was a place at our rental property where cattle and goats would come through, so I decided that putting up a screen to deter them was a good idea. I also decided it would be fun to film it and share the project with my YouTube viewers.

I made a mistake when I first planted the hedge, however, and used branches from a *Gliricidia* lookalike. They completely failed to root, and a farmer friend pointed out my error, then helped me find some actual *Gliricidia* branches. I tore out the old fence, then planted the new branches. Then I filmed another video sharing my mistake and showing *Gliricidia* and its lookalike side-by-side. The second time, the branches took almost immediately and quickly grew into a dense screen.

Then we moved. When I went back to check on the progress of my hedge a few months ago, I found the landlord had ripped it all out. Well, so much for that.

I write all this to let you know there is no shame in failure. It's better to attempt and fail than never to attempt at all. Hey, no one is perfect. And I did learn a few things from the experiment.

1. Planting on someone else's land is pointless

2. *Gliricidia* roots quickly and makes a good screen

3. Improper plant ID makes you look like an idiot on YouTube

I'm going to attempt the project again now that I'm on my own land. This time I will get to watch how it grows over time and see if the tied stems will graft themselves together into a living lattice.

Stay tuned.

If you're not sure if a plant will root by jamming a branch in the ground—I mean, carefully inserting a branch into a perfect pre-dug hole—then try it and see. Watering is key with these experiments, because if you try something but don't give it any care, you won't really know if it was possible or not. It's like marrying a gal then neglecting her completely, then when she leaves you decide the problem was our culture of divorce or feminism or gluten or something. Just give a little ongoing care and things will work out much better.

Rooting Cuttings in Water

This is one of the most common beginner methods for rooting cuttings. You cut a piece off a plant, then stick it in a jar of water where it grows roots, then when you have plenty of roots, you plant it in soil.

Some plants are really easy to start this way, like every ivy I've ever known, but other plants just rot. It seems that plants with more succulent stems root more easily in water than plants with woody stems. Try this on some things and you just end up with rotten stems and stinking water. I will take cuttings and stick them in water until I get the chance to put them in soil, but usually I don't keep them in water to root. I've had too many failures. It may be the easiest method, but it's not the best. Unless you want lots of ivy.

Leaf Cuttings

Some leaves will actually root, no stem required. When I was a kid I remember my Grandma rooting African violet leaves. She would carefully cut one leaf from the plant and stick it in its own little pot. Some time later, a tiny little plant would appear where the petiole was stuck in the soil. It's amazing to see a new plant growing from a single leaf. This only works with some plants, namely those with the ability to produce what are called "adventitious buds". This means that the plant can create roots and shoots from just about anywhere. With African violets, you stick the petiole in the soil and let the rest of the leaf stay above the ground, but you can do something even weirder with begonias.

That's like some sort of horror show! You cut through some of the veins in the leaves, then pin the leaf down to some moist soil and put it in a mini-greenhouse, then watch. In a short time, tiny little begonia plants will start springing from the damaged areas. It looks so weird it doesn't seem real—but it is. Sadly, this doesn't work with most plants so you're not likely to get much mileage from the method, but it is pretty darn cool.

Root Cuttings

With root cuttings, you take a piece of a plant's root from the ground in the right season (mid-to-late fall to mid-winter in temperate climates), lay it in a growing medium, cover it with a little more medium, then put it in the greenhouse until it starts growing. This works well on some species and not at all on many others.

As the Royal Horticultural Society notes:

Herbaceous plants that take well from root cuttings often have thick or fleshy roots. Some plants, such as Papaver *and* Primula denticulata, *do not take from shoot cuttings, although they will grow well from root cuttings.*

A range of herbaceous plants can be propagated from root cuttings. These include Acanthus, Anemone hupehensis,

Split vein leaf propagation of begonias

A. x hybrida, B
Phlox, Primula denticu

*Also, a few woody plants can be p
such as Aesculus parviflora, Ailanthus, Ai
dian bean tree),* Chaenomeles, Clerodendrum, A
Sophora *and* Syringa *(lilac) and climbers such as* Campsis
Passiflora *(passion flower) and* Solanum. *

This method also works well for breadfruit. Sometimes people will just chop at the roots around the base of a breadfruit tree, which causes the tree to pop up suckers which can then be transplanted. If you have a plant that likes to sucker, chances are decent it will propagate from root cuttings.

Tubers

The previous type of root cutting is different than the way you can cut up potatoes or yams to make more plants, as you're using regular old roots and not a nice, fat tuber. Propagation from tubers is much easier. Some tubers can root from almost any place whereas others do not. Potatoes have specific spots where the "eyes" sprout, as does ginger. True yams (*Dioscorea spp.*) don't really have noticeable eyes and seem to root all over the place. Sweet potatoes tend to sprout all towards one end and some botanists don't consider them tubers, rather naming them

---

* https://www.rhs.org.uk/advice/profile?pid=407

...ect everyone on ...y can see how smart you ...e tuberous species in Chapter 7.

...ngs

...nts such as cacti, jade plant, pencil tree and other plants more adapted for dry environments really don't like being wet and often benefit from drying out a little before being planted. If you just cut them and stick them in soil, some species rot instead of root. Take cuttings, let the sap dry over on the cut portion, then stick them into slightly moist potting mix without making a mini-greenhouse. They don't need or want the humidity. Just put the cuttings into pots and wait. I've had luck just sticking cactus pads part-way into the ground where I want them to grow, no nursery time required.

Air Layering

When you air layer a plant, you actually leave a branch on the tree and trick it into producing roots. When I was a kid, I read about this method in Stan DeFreitas' book *Florida Gardening*, then went and tried it on an orange tree in my Grandpa's back yard. To my surprise, it worked. Unfortunately, once I cut off the rooted branch and planted it, I didn't water it enough and it died. Live and learn. When you take really good care of it, it is imperative that you take really good care of it until it has the root capacity to thrive under more neglect.

Air layering takes mo
it allows you to grow a new pla
mother, meaning that you can start the
walk away for a few months, then come back
tree or shrub.

Pick a relatively new section of stem. A couple of years
or less is perfect. Find a branch, then cut off all but the main
shoot you plan to propagate with a pair of sharp clippers, then
make a pair of shallow cuts into the branch up to two feet or
so from the end, at about an inch apart. Just cut through the
bark layer, and peel that strip of bark right off between the cuts.
Dust the area with rooting hormone, then pack a handful of
well-soaked sphagnum moss around the stem and wrap that in
plastic, sealing up the ends with rubber bands, tape or zip ties.

You can also just wrap aluminum foil around the plastic to
keep it in place. Now leave it alone for at least a few months. It
might even take as long as a year to root, but you can come back
and check on it every few months to see what's happening. Just
look and see if roots are starting to fill up the plastic. When you
see a nice bundle of strong roots, cut the branch a little below
the wounded area and pot your new plant. Don't go picking
at the moss or whatever you used—you don't want to damage
the roots! Be gentle and pot it carefully, then keep it watered. I
recommend putting the new plant in some shade to lower the
stress on it. Though sphagnum moss is the usual medium used
for air layering, I have had luck with other things in a pinch.

Stripped bark on mango branch in preparation for air layering

Ziploc bag of substrate wrapped around wounded mango branch

Coconut coir is regularly used in [...]
clay work.

Some trees will take easily this way, whereas [...]
want to root. Sometimes it may just be operator err[...]
rooting branches from my Grandpa's mango tree with some[...]
layers a few years ago and had no luck, but I've seen multiple
videos from India where gardeners have great luck with mangoes. If you aren't sure whether a tree is a good air layering
candidate or not, there's no harm in trying, as all you lose is a
little time and a small tree branch.

Ground Layering

Even easier than air layering is ground layering. This method
can be as simple as taking a low-growing branch of a shrub or
tree, then bending it down to the ground so you can bury a
portion of it, and putting a rock on top to keep it in place as it
roots.

For better results, wound the branch with a knife and put
some rooting hormone on the cut. Growers often use what
look like big wire staples to hold a branch down in the ground.
Feel free to improvise however you like. Cutting and bending
a wire clothes hanger should work well.

Mound Layering

This is a method of plant propagation most people outside
the nursery trade have never seen. It's a way of producing a

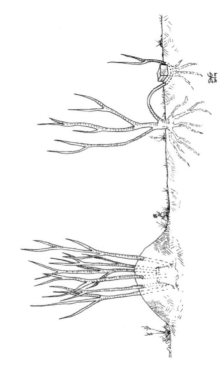

Left to right: mound layering and ground layering

bunch of cloned plants from one tree. The [...] Extension Service explains it thus:

> *Mound layering is useful with heavy-stemmed, [...] branched shrubs, like Spirea, Flowering Quince, or Magnolia. It is also useful for fruit root stock production. The original plant may be cut back to encourage many new shoots to grow from the base. Then, the following spring after the new shoots have grown approximately 8–10 inches, mound soil containing sphagnum peat moss about 7–9 inches deep around the shrub. Roots will grow into the surrounding soil from the new growth. The following autumn or spring, gently dig into the mound, separate and transplant the new plants.* [*]

If you've ever cut down a tree and seen a bunch of shoots come back from the trunk, you've done the first part of this process. All you're doing is mounding a growing medium over the base of those shoots so they start rooting.

If you divide them off during their winter dormancy, you have bare-root trees which can be transplanted into pots or directly to where you'd like them to grow.

Tip Layering

Tip layering is very much like ground layering, except you bury the entire tip of a shoot into the ground and let it root. Eventually, it sends up growth and sends up roots, then can be cut off

[*] https://ag.purdue.edu/hla/pubs/HO/HO-1-W.pdf

—or left in place. This works really well

planted a a couple of blackberry plants, then stuck .ple tips into the ground as the plants grew. Over a few years, I had filled over a hundred square feet with blackberries, all from those two little plants. Bury the top of a shoot in the ground and a rooted plant will grow there. Easy as blackberry pie. I have seen people do this with hedges, too, expanding their hedge in a row, one tip layer at a time.

Division

Speaking of easy, propagation doesn't get any easier than division. This works well for most plants with a clumping habit. Just stick a shovel through the middle of a clump, dig out half the clump (or however much you want) and plant that part elsewhere.

You can often divide a big clump into a bunch of individual plants. I've done this with lilies, gingers, grasses, bamboo and lots more. If you have a clumping plant, chances are you can divide the clump to make more plants. Easy!

But enough about cuttings. Let's get into the not-so-scary world of grafting.

5

Lose Your Fear and Get Grafting

What is the point of grafting? I mean, when people say that a tree can be propagated by "grafting", what does that actually mean? Isn't grafting just taking a piece from one plant and sticking it on to another?

Yes, but it's more than that. It's like a two-part method of propagation, and it allows you to do some very interesting and entertaining things.

The first part required for grafting is the rootstock. This is what it sounds like—it's the part of the new plant that bears the roots. The second part is the bud or the scion, which will be the entire top of the plant above the graft. It's what exhibits the flowers, fruits, variegation or whatever else you're looking for, and it's the exact clone of whatever the donor tree or shrub happened to be. If you have a Gala apple planted in the ground and you cut off the trunk at 15" and graft a Granny Smith onto the trunk, you will now have a tree that bears Granny Smith apples, not Gala apples—and not a cross between the two. They are two distinct individuals which have been joined into one. The leaves and fruit are Granny Smith leaves and fruit, and they feed the roots below with their photosynthesizing, and the roots in turn supply them with water and minerals and support.

But it's actually more complicated than that, because if you are growing any Gala apple, it's already a grafted apple, unless you somehow rooted a Gala branch and planted it. There is only one set of genetics that equal "Gala", and all Galas—except for the original seedling in New Zealand, if it still exists—are clones grafted on top of rootstocks. The rootstocks are often clones themselves, though some are grown from seed. That means you have three distinct individuals in that one tree. The rootstock is one thing, the stem between the original graft and the new Granny Smith graft is a Gala apple, and the top of the tree above the graft is all Granny Smith.

Whew.

Okay, so now that you're totally confused, let's talk about the rootstock and simplify things a little. A rootstock is usually selected for its strength, its dwarfing ability, its resistance to diseases or multiple other factors, sometimes all at the same time. One popular rootstock for stone fruit is called "Nemaguard" because of its resistance to nematodes, which are a common pest, particularly in peaches.

UC Davis has a profile on this that shares its pros and cons, noting that it was:

Selected from seedlings from a seedlot received in 1949 by the US Department of Agriculture (USDA), which was labeled P. davidiana *and was eventually released as 'FV 234-1' in 1959 (Brooks and Olmo, 1961).—Refer to link in DESCRIPTION field. Precocious. In NC-140 Trials: 1984, 2001. Main rootstock used in California because it is resistant to root-knot nematode and is compatible with peach, nectarine and plum. It makes a vigorous, productive tree with good fruit size. However, it does not tolerate waterlogged or calcareous soils and is susceptible to many soil pests including ring nematode, verticillium wilt, bacterial canker and armillaria.[*]*

The variety is propagated by seeds, meaning that it's been bred to be true to type. The Nemaguard peach makes peaches, but they are not a commercial type and are used for planting material.

Some rootstocks help keep a tree smaller and these are known as "dwarfing" rootstocks. Fruit trees often come in Dwarf, Semi-Dwarf and Standard sizes. Standard trees are usually longer-lived and bear a lot more, but they may not easily fit into an orchard are yard and aren't usually preferred. I believe you can do a lot with pruning so I'm happy to grow "standard" trees, but a lot of people would rather let the rootstock do it for them.

Once you have your rootstock, you have the bottom of your

---

[*] http://fps.ucdavis.edu/treedetails.cfm?v=1045

tree. For the top, you pick something you like and graft it on. If you want a Red Delicious apple or a Navel orange or an Elberta peach, you take some wood and graft it on to your rootstock and this gets you exactly the fruit you want, every single time. Seedling trees have a diversity of genetics. This means you might get something great, or you might get something lousy. There is uncertainty there and grafting eliminates it.

If you plant a mango pit, you don't know if you're going to get great fruit. If you don't want to wait and find out, you can just graft on some scion wood from a tree you know makes good fruit, then you'll have that tree growing in your yard. It will bear exactly the same good fruit as the tree from which you took the scion wood.

There's another benefit to grafting over seedlings, and that is the time to bear. Trees often have an extended juvenile period where they grow without producing anything. Mulberries can take a decade to produce fruit from seed. Apples can take 6–10 years. When you take scion wood from a mature tree, however, the resulting tree produces much faster. This is why you see two-foot-tall lime trees fruiting in their pots at Home Depot. They think they're a big tree already! If that had been a seedling lime, it might be eight feet tall and four years old before blooming.

Grafting allows you to shortcut—literally cut!—the normal life cycle of a tree and get fruit quickly while also ensuring that you get exactly the fruit you want. I find growing trees from seed a lot of fun and I enjoy the genetic diversity, but grafting saves time and eliminates uncertainty, which is why commercial growers always use grafted trees in their orchards.

It's really an amazing thing. You can have a white rose in your yard, cut it back, then graft on pink or yellow or red roses—or all three—and transform it completely. You can also leave white roses on one branch and add red to another.

Another thing about grafting is it can let you grow fruit trees in marginal areas by taking advantage of hardy rootstocks.

I once did a horticultural analysis of a property way out in the scrublands. The owner had good clean water, no real neighbors, a great location—and hot, fast-drying, mineral-poor sand that was really, really bad for gardening.

There was no couching it. I had to tell him: this area is very poor for gardening and your project ideas are going to take a lot of work. Pulling off a vegetable garden is tough when your soil will barely support much in the way of fruit or nut trees.

What the land did have was a decent amount of native American persimmon trees (*Diospyros virginiana*). They were dwarfed by drought and stress, but they were strong and alive. That said, I saw very few with fruit.

It was a start. Native persimmons have a few drawbacks, though. Unlike their cultivated Japanese persimmon (*Diospyros kaki*) relations, they're dioecious. That means you have male and female trees—and you need both to get fruit. The male won't make fruit but it does provide the pollen that allows the females to fruit.

Japanese persimmons are self-fertile, plus they make hefty, sweet fruit. They're also regularly grafted onto American persimmon rootstock.

Seeing the wild trees gave me an idea: why not use the existing trees as rootstocks for Japanese persimmons? They were already established and growing in poor soil, making them a perfect support for a higher-producing and delicious variety of improved persimmon.

This is why you should really think hard before cutting down any trees or plants. Our first observations aren't the best. You might see a crabapple with lousy fruit in your yard and think "I hate that thing! I'll tear it out and plant a good apple in its place!" I've seen this again and again. People will cut down a big and healthy sour orange tree and then plant a Navel in its place. Though there's nothing wrong with preferring sweet oranges to sour, that isn't the point. The point is that they could have saved years of waiting for sweet oranges by hijacking the root system of the sour orange and using it to grow sweet oranges. When you graft on to an established tree, you get fruit fast. It took years to build that root system—take advantage of it!

Step back and think about the trees you don't like or prefer. Want to change them? If they have relatives or cultivars you like, perhaps you can just spend a few minutes grafting and give the tree a total makeover. With grafting you can go nip some twigs off good apple trees, graft them onto a crabapple, then voila—in a year or two you'll be getting sweet apples instead of crabapples.

Like those stupid ornamental pears people grow for the blooms. Did you know you can graft real pears onto them? There are folks doing that in California right now by illegally "guerrilla grafting" street trees. Doesn't that change the landscape a bit? Ornamental trees are mostly a non-productive liability whereas productive trees are a serious asset. Since you already have to rake and pick up fallen branches, might as well get some fruit while you're at it. If you've got ornamental pears, plums, peaches, apples, etc., why not switch them up by grafting on some good varieties?

At the same property where I saw the American persimmon trees, I also came across quite a few hawthorns. After reading you could graft pears onto some hawthorn trees, I added a few scions to them—and they took. Now that super-hardy hawthorn rootstock will bear pear fruit instead of tiny little hawthorn fruit.

My old neighborhood in North Florida had wild persimmons growing here and there around the block. Some of these are on empty lots and in unused property with absentee owners. Wild persimmon fruit is only found on 50% of the trees (since the other half are male). That fruit is about 1" in diameter, plus it's astringent and seedy.

I had Japanese persimmons in my yard that made sweet fruit as large as a beefsteak tomato and just as delicious (if not more so).

Though the legalities are rather gray, I don't think anyone

would really mind if I had taken buds off my Japanese persimmon tree and grafted them into the wild trees here and there around the neighborhood. People would find it rather puzzling, sure—but be upset by it? I doubt it. Heck, at the very worst all I've done is improve somebody's tree. And I've put food where there wasn't food.

And here's something really weird. If you want American persimmons (which can be quite good, despite my picking on them) but you only have a male or a female in your yard without a pollinator, guess what? You can do a sex change on one branch—or the whole tree—with grafting.

Say you have a female tree but it isn't bearing. Go find a male tree, then graft on a few pieces of scion wood on a few branches of the female tree. The tree will then bloom and self-pollinate, producing pollen on the male branches and fruit on the female ones.

In your local woods you may have quite a few trees growing which could be judiciously improved, turning them into fruit-production machines rather than marginally useful wild specimens.

Grafting also allows you to get more varieties of fruit into your yard.

My friend Steven Edholm worked for years on an apple tree he calls Frankentree, which is truly an apple-producing monster. He found a tough rootstock, then started grafting:

The owner planted an Arkansas black apple some years back, but the top must have died and only the rootstock survived because the apples were small hard green things not fit for eating. Not if you're a spoiled human anyway. One day I found 4 to 6 inch claw marks covering one side of the tree up to 4 feet and more. Long curls of bark hung from the scratches. A few broken branches near the top told the story of a bear climbing the tree to get at the fruit. When I first saw this tree I was very excited because in spite of receiving no care whatsoever beyond establishment it was putting on good yearly growth and looked healthy and vigorous. I figured maybe some of the trees I intended to plant in the future might do this well without excessive pampering and was happy. Since the apples were useless I went straight away to the Scion exchange and collected a large pile of scions to work the tree over to different varieties. Every year in early to mid march Tamara and I go out to the !Frankentree! to add more varieties. I graft the scions onto the tree and she makes labels and takes notes to keep track of what we put on and when. As of today there are 84 distinct varieties (now 140), several unknowns from which the tags were lost or never put on and a few repeats. [*]

Obviously that's an extreme case, but you can easily add a half-dozen varieties of fruit to a single tree with grafting.

---

[*] http://skillcult.com/blog/2010/03/16/113

If you've seen "fruit cocktail" trees for sale in the local nursery, that's how they did it. It's a multi-grafted tree. If you need two different types of apple for pollination purposes, you can just graft them both onto one tree and you'll have apples. You can also get a much longer harvest from one tree by grafting early, mid-season and late apples all onto one rootstock. You'll save space as well. If I only had a tiny yard, I would totally go Frankentree in it. Heck, even with a big yard it's worth doing for fun.

I had a native Chickasaw plum tree growing in my North Florida food forest and it became ground zero for my grafting experiments a few years ago. The first thing I tried was adding a European plum variety to it. I didn't know if it would work, because they look very different. The Chickasaw plum is a little weedy-looking tree with reddish bark and small, usually sour fruits, whereas the European plums have light bark and thicker trunks, with big sweet fruit.

In one year the little scion I grafted on grew into a 5' branch. Obviously, it was happy with the Chickasaw rootstock.

After seeing the graft succeed, I had a conversation with Paul Miller of Rainbow Star Farm in Gainesville. For three-plus decades, he was in charge of the fruit tree breeding program at UF. The man knows his stuff.

I told him about my successful graft and he congratulated me, then told me something very, very interesting. He shared that the Chickasaw plum is a "universal" rootstock for more than just other plums, and that it would also support peaches, nectarines, apricots and potentially even cherries.

The problem, he told me, was that the Chickasaw plum trees are very flexible and do not grow nearly as large as many of the trees you can graft onto it. That means that above the graft you might end up with a large tree top that will bow the lower Chickasaw trunk down to the ground. In order to fix this, he told me to simply knock a fence pole into the ground and tie the tree up.

It was all true. The first branch I had grafted was already pulling the tree down. It was grafted onto just one of the many suckering stems made by the tree and was definitely heading down to the ground unless I did something. I rammed a piece of electrical conduit into the ground and tied up the trunk. The next year I grafted on more plums, plus I added peaches and nectarines, which all took. I also tried some sweet cherry wood but it failed.

All the grafts grew insanely fast, and just a year after I grafted on that first plum branch, it bloomed and bore me a dozen delicious fruits. Seeing how easy it was to graft onto wild Chickasaw plums, I surreptitiously grafted a peach scion onto a wild plum hanging over the fence in a neighbor's lot—and it took. Now there's a peach branch growing over the road.

So why would you want to bother with grafting onto a weedy little tree like the Chickasaw if you have to support the branches afterwards?

For one thing, the Chickasaw plum is a super tough little tree. It manages lousy soil, nematodes, drought and all kinds of other stresses without flinching. It's hard to say the same for improved fruit trees.

For another thing, Chickasaw plums pop up all over the place, thanks to birds dropping the seeds around. If you're in an area where Chickasaw plums grow in the woods near your place, you're likely to have them show up in the yard if you quit mowing. All those seedlings with their nice, tough root systems, can just be converted into good fruit-bearing trees. If nature gives you seedlings, splice on some scions!

On the downside, the Chickasaw plum is a prolific creator of suckers. They'll form a thicket in no time if you don't stay on top of them. Of course, there's nothing keeping you from grafting additional peaches, nectarines and plums onto those suckers and making a home-grown thicket of edible fruit.

You can also just mow down the suckers you don't want. Taking advantage of its excellent root system by tacking on better fruit makes a lot of sense.

And this is just one example among many. The trifoliate orange is an almost inedible citrus, yet it is a very common rootstock for good edible varieties due to how tough and cold-tolerant it is. Pecan can be grafted onto hickory. Loquats can allegedly be grafted onto pyracantha, among other very strange grafting possibilities. *Plant Breeding Reviews*, Volume 37 relates:

*There are reports of other rosaceous species being evaluated as rootstocks for loquat in various countries. These include hawthorn (*Cratagous scabrifolia Rehd.*), apple (*Malus x domestica Horkh.*), fire-thorn (*Pyracantha fortuneana Roem.*), medlar (*Mespilus vulgaris Rchb.*, pear (*Pyrus communis L.*), Chinese photinia (*Phatinia sernzlato Lind.*), and quince (*Cydonia oblonga Mill.*). Quince and pyracantha rootstocks may cause extreme scion dwarfing. Dwarfing on quince rootstocks has encouraged expansion of loquat cultivation in Israel since 1960. Quince rootstocks selections (A, C, BA29) produce smaller, more compact trees, a shorter juvenile period, and larger fruits with high sugar content and good color.*[*]

Some things just won't graft though. I've had people ask things like "Can I graft avocados onto mangoes?" or "Can I graft pear branches onto my holly tree?"

No, you can't. The easiest grafts are ones inside the same family. For instance, grafting one type of apple onto another. The next easiest are inside the same genus. Like grafting cultivated pear onto a wild pear. Or grafting a cultivated plum (*Prunus domestica*) onto a wild Chickasaw plum (*Prunus angustifolia*). Some of these interspecies grafts will take, others will not. Some crosses don't work which you think would work—and others between even less related species will work.

---

[*] https://hort.purdue.edu/newcrop/pdfs/breeding-loquat-pbr37.pdf

For example, you can graft pears (*Pyrus spp.*) onto quince (*Cydonia oblonga*). They are both in the *Rosaceae* family, but they're not even in the same genus.

Yet I tried grafting sweet cherry (*Prunus avium*) onto black cherry (*Prunus serotina*)—both of which are cherries and in the same genus—and all my attempts failed.

Just know that the more closely related your rootstock and your scion are, the more likely it is that your graft will work.

Now that we know more of the *why* and the *what* of grafting, let's allay any fears you may harbor about grafting and jump into the *how*.

Grafting is Easy

I know what many of you are thinking: "All the above mad scientist stuff is nice, Dave, but I don't know how to graft trees!"

I understand that feeling. I was in your shoes for a long time. Grafting was something that seemed complicated. Planting beans? No big deal. Drying fruit? Easy. Grafting? OMIGOSHNO! THAT LOOKS HARD!

It's not, though. Sure, it takes a little whittling experience and a couple of decent tools but it isn't really hard. Think of it as transplanting one tree on top of another. You just need to match up two pieces of wood and stick them together until they heal, that's all. And like cuttings, you need to make sure the grafts don't dry out. All easy.

And it's more useful than you might think at first glance. I once saved the genetics of an improved loquat tree girdled by a string trimmer by grafting some of its buds onto some seedling loquats. If your favorite apple tree gets knocked down by a storm or a runaway dump truck, you can take pieces of it and quickly graft them onto another apple tree to preserve the variety.

Don't worry about messing up when you graft. We all mess up. There's no harm in trying something new. It looks complicated but it isn't. If you can slice carrots and tape them together again, you can graft.

Get yourself a sharp pocketknife or a utility knife, some pruning shears, a roll of grafting tape, grafting compound and your courage… then start grafting. I filmed a full instructional video back in 2016 demonstrating three easy grafting methods. If you want to see how to do it, go look that up. It's on YouTube for free and it's entitled "Get Grafting!"

As you graft and build skills, you'll get a feel for it and it won't be hard any more. Just do it. As an example, in 2015 I went on a grafting binge and kept track of what worked and what didn't work:

Worked:

- Nectarine grafts onto Chickasaw plum

- Peach grafts onto Chickasaw plum

- Improved plums graft onto Chickasaw plum

- Black mulberry onto black mulberry

- Orient pear onto Kieffer pear

- Thanksgiving pear onto Kieffer pear

- Various apple onto apple

- Peach onto Bruce plum

- Nectarine onto seedling peach

- Texas Everbearing fig onto unknown yellow fig (one took, one failed)

- Pear onto wild hawthorn

Failed:

- Brown Turkey fig onto black mulberry

- Minnie Royal cherry onto wild black cherry

- Minnie Royal cherry onto Chickasaw plum

- Long mulberry onto black mulberry

- Black mulberry onto paper mulberry

Alright, now it's your turn.

Here are the three keys to successful grafting.

Make Nice Cuts with a Clean, Sharp Knife

I sterilize my grafting knife with alcohol before grafting and between grafts. You are wounding the plant and getting bacteria and dirt into a wound is bad news. Whittling away isn't a good thing, either. Practice your cuts to make them as precise as you can manage. Less damage = a higher success rate. I like to do most of my grafting with a razor utility knife with a new blade. I also carry a bottle of cheap vodka with me to both sterilize the blade in between cuts and give myself courage to graft.

Line up the Cambium

The second key to successful grafting is you must line up the cambium layer in your scion wood with the cambium layer of your rootstock.

The US Forest Service defines the cambium layer as:

> … *the growing part of the trunk. It annually produces new bark and new wood in response to hormones that pass down through the phloem with food from the leaves. These hormones, called 'auxins', stimulate growth in cells. Auxins are produced by leaf buds at the ends of branches as soon as they start growing in spring.*[*]

The cambium layer is just under the bark. You'll see it when you cut a branch, right between the bark on the outside and the

---

[*] https://www.fs.fed.us/learn/trees/anatomy-of-tree

wood on the inside. When you graft on a piece of wood and the cambium from the rootstock and the scion touch, they grow together and the movement of sap and growth hormones takes place and the area will join and heal over. It's astounding to see how a graft will heal together and join two plants into one. The cambium layer doesn't even have to touch all the way around the graft—just having a piece of it touch is often enough for the graft to heal and grow together.

If you make a graft and the cambium is misaligned, it will fail. It doesn't matter how nice and tight the connection feels, the cambium layers must touch or it's a bad graft.

Don't Let It Dry Out

The third key to grafting success is ensuring the graft does not dry out. As with cuttings, grafts often fail though inadequate moisture. I wrap my grafts tightly with flagging tape and usually paint them with a wound sealer to keep the air from drying out my scion. If I have parafilm, which is a waxy, stretchy, grafting tape, I will do the graft, then wrap the entire scion from below the graft point up and over the top bud. The buds can grow right through the tape and the tape keeps moisture in.

If you align the cambium, use a sharp, clean blade, and keep the graft from drying out, your success rates will be much better than if you hack at your tree with a greasy steak knife, jam it together willy-nilly, then don't do anything to protect the graft.

Now you need to pick your rootstock and decide what you're going to do with it. Are you hoping to add some new varieties to a tree or are you going to replace the entire top of the tree with a new variety? In my nursery, I would pot up seedlings and then cut them off at a foot or so high, removing the entire top of the tree, then graft in a new variety. Or I would add a side-veneer graft without cutting the tree back, then once it took, cut the top of the tree off. Now it was the variety I wanted and I could let it grow for a while and offer it for sale.

Once you know what you want to do, you need to get your scion wood. For temperate species, the best time to gather scion wood and do your grafting is a little before the trees wake up in spring. If you're grafting tropical species, it's a little trickier and you need to look for scion wood that isn't actively growing. Catch it in between growth spurts and you'll have much better luck.

I clip scion wood from dormant temperate trees and put it in a plastic bag, then store them in my fridge until I'm ready to graft. You can keep them for a month or more this way—they are dead asleep and don't seem to notice they've been cut from their roots. I also like to add on a label when I graft so I don't lose track of what is what. If I don't name the variety by hanging a little tag on the branch, I will forget what I've done. I prefer

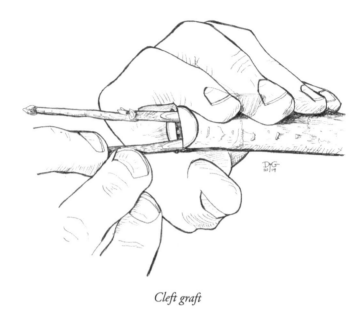

Cleft graft

the aluminum tags you can write on with a pencil, leaving an indentation that doesn't fade in the sun.

Now it's time to actually graft.

I generally stick to four main grafts. The cleft graft, the wedge graft, the side veneer graft and the whip-and-tongue graft, though there are a bunch more you can try.

The Cleft Graft

With cleft grafting, you take a large rootstock and graft in two smaller scions of around 3/8" in diameter, with 3–4 buds each. 4–6" long scions will work great. This technique is very useful for top-working, where you want to completely remake a mature existing tree into a different cultivar. In late winter or early spring when both your scion wood and your rootstock are dormant, pick the tree you want to graft and you saw off a branch or the entire trunk, then saw or use a wedge to make a cleft a couple inches deep into the trunk or branch. Then tap a wedge into the cleft to hold the trunk apart so you can add your scions. The scions need to be carefully trimmed on both sides so they fit the angle of the cleft, then inserted so the cambium on one side of the scion touches the cambium towards the outer edge of the cleft.

Make sure that the scion cuts are nice and even so they take. Precision is key. Don't worry about matching up the bark, as the bark on the tree will be a lot thicker than the bark on your scion. Just match the cambium layer.

Once you have your two scions in place, remove the wedge holding open the cleft. The pressure of the split should hold the scion wood in place just fine if you've done it right. Now paint the whole thing with tree wound sealer or grafting wax to keep in moisture.

When the tree breaks dormancy, the scions should start growing. Once they do, pick your favorite and cut away the other one so the tree can heal.

This is a riskier graft but it's a great way to take a big tree and change it into another variety.

As I write this, I have a Jin Huang mango scion sitting in a glass of water on my counter, waiting for me to graft it onto a mango seedling growing on my land. I nipped it off a friend's tree yesterday and when I graft it this evening, I will use a cleft graft as the rootstock is a bit thicker than my scion wood.

The Wedge Graft

To make things a little confusing, this graft is also sometimes called a "cleft" graft, though I stick to calling it the wedge graft to differentiate it from the graft above, which involves tacking smaller scions onto a larger rootstock. With the wedge graft, you match up a scion with a rootstock of comparable diameter, then cut a long, sharp wedge into your scion, matched to a slice of the same depth into the rootstock. Join them up and then tie up with tape and paint with wound sealer, or cover in parafilm.

The wedge graft is a very simple graft that can be performed by anyone.

I visited a local government plant propagation station last week and saw that the wedge graft was the graft they were using for sapodillas and mangoes.

The Side Veneer Graft

The side veneer graft allows you to add a scion without cutting off—at first—the main part of the tree.

This is really a good graft for loquats. I originally learned it from my friend Oliver Moore who is much better at it than I am. Some years ago he gave me a variety of improved loquat.

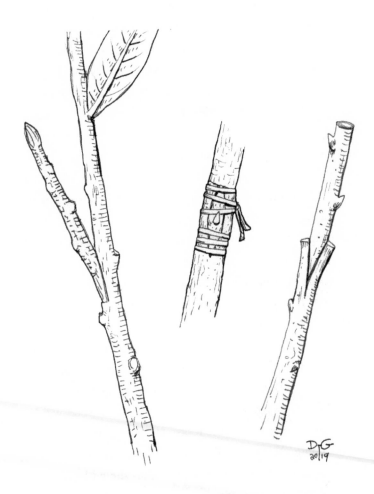

Left to right: Side veneer graft, bud graft and wedge graft

Quite a lot of the loquats you see are seedling varieties which are often planted as a landscape tree because they're beautiful and evergreen. The seedling varieties usually make somewhat sour fruits, though they're often pretty good, especially for chutney. It's usually a decent fruit no matter whether it's a seedling or not, but the improved varieties are much bigger and/or sweeter. Since loquats always have leaves, even in winter, when you graft them it's important to get scion wood that isn't soft or actively growing. Get ones that have buds on the end that are swollen and getting ready to grow but aren't leafing out yet, then nip off the side leaves below the bud. Every leaf is a place that water can escape. Side veneer grafts are also great for mangoes and you follow the same procedure as with loquats.

If you're grafting other types of fruit trees that are dormant, you won't have any leaves so it's even easier.

With side veneer grafting, you usually graft on to young seedlings, not mature trees. It's a common graft in the nursery business. If it fails, the tree will heal and keep growing and you can try again since you're not cutting off the entire top. Unlike the cleft graft, with side veneer grafts the scion wood will be closer to the diameter of the rootstock, though it doesn't have to match up. You can graft a somewhat smaller piece of scion wood onto a larger rootstock. Your scions should be about 6" long.

Pick a spot on the side of your rootstock and cut down, separating a thin 2" or so "veneer" piece of bark and cambium, right against the inner wood of the tree. Now slice all the way down one side of your scion to match the bare spot on the rootstock, then cut an angled piece off the other side to fit in against the peeled down piece of rootstock bark. Match the two pieces together, then wrap up some parafilm or flagging tape from the bottom to join them, making sure the scion's cambium is lining up with the rootstock and is nice and tight. Then wrap down from the top again. I cover the entire graft with parafilm or grafting compound so it doesn't dry out.

Also, if you don't feel like you made a very good cut and you think that it's not sticking together all that well, you can always cheat it by taking a little bit of your flagging tape and tying it around and really pulling it tight to cinch up the connection. Don't worry, the grafting police aren't going to come for you.

Without about two weeks, the grafted portion should start growing. Nip off any buds that try to grow beneath the graft so the rootstock doesn't take over, then once the graft really looks like it's taken—usually after a month or so—cut off the top of the rootstock just above the graft and let the scion take over.

If you are grafting in the field, you don't have control over the sun, but if you're grafting onto a potted tree, I would keep it out of full sun until the graft has taken and is growing nicely.

The Whip-and-Tongue Graft

I really like this graft. It's a classic, though it takes a little skill to get the cuts right.

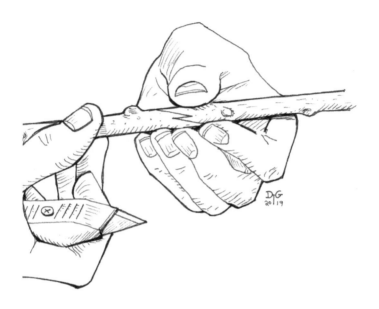

Whip and tongue graft

I don't recommend you just go outside and try this one without doing a few practice runs first. To do that, go nip a few little branches off a peach or an apple or whatever fruit tree you please, sticking to about 3/8" diameter pieces. Then sit on the porch and cut the diagonal cuts and the little tongues in two different pieces and match them together, pretending one piece is the scion and the other is the rootstock. They'll hold together all on their own if you do it right.

Once you have a little confidence, it's time to go out and try it for real. I used this graft to add various stone fruit to my Chickasaw plum tree. With the whip-and-tongue, you really need to get the same diameter scion and rootstock so they match nicely. Cut the angle and the tongue in both pieces, then put them tightly together and wrap up with tape, then wither wrap parafilm around the entire scion or paint it with wound sealer. Usually they take in a couple of weeks. Longer than that and it's probably a failed graft.

I did a lot of apples and pears this way, as well as mulberries and figs.

Bud Grafting

This graft is commonly used for citrus. Instead of taking a piece of twig with a few buds on it, you simply cut off a dormant bud—one single little slice!—from the tree you want, then cut a 'T' into the bark of your desired rootstock and slip the bud in, then wrap over the graft until it heals.

Once it heals up a few weeks later, you can then cut off the rootstock above the graft, which causes the tree to start sending growth hormones up the stem, activating your bud and making it grow. Voila! The top growth of your tree is now your desired variety.

It's not the easiest thing to do but it's also not brain surgery. It's important that the rootstock is actively growing and not totally dormant. You can tell if the tree will properly receive a bud when you peel back the bark. If it "slips", you're good. If not, wait. Budding can be done all summer, weather permitting, so it's a good graft to learn in case you miss your normal late winter/spring grafting season.

You should use a really sharp blade to do this graft properly. It's also important to make sure the new growth is protected from damage, as it's just one bud coming from the side of the rootstock and it's really easy to have the growing shoot knocked off when it's green, especially with citrus.

It's not necessary to know bud grafting if you have citrus, as you can also use other methods, but bud grafting does allow you to graft with a lot less donor material as you're just using single buds, hence its popularity in the nursery business.

Final Thoughts on Grafting

Once you practice and perform a few successful grafts, you are off to the races. It's fun to see what works and to add varieties to existing trees. It's also fun eating fruit a lot faster than you would if you simply planted seeds.

There are a wide range of grafting techniques—enough for a complete book on the topic—but once you have whip and tongue, cleft, and side veneer, with the possible addition of bud grafting, you can pretty much graft anything.

So get out there and get grafting!

6

Find Plants and Make Them Yours

When you are a plant lover, the world is a very distracting place. I was driving a sailor friend back to his boat recently and spotted a beautiful *Barringtonia* tree across from a gas station. I had been told the tree was there but hadn't seen it in person.

"Wait a minute!" I said to my friend. "There's a tree here I have to see!"

I looked around for a parking spot but didn't find anything handy, so I parked alongside the drive into a commercial building in a less-than-legal fashion. "Here!" I said, "I'll leave the car running—I have to go look at the *Barringtonia*! If anyone gets on your case, just move the car!"

Much to my delight, I was able to grab five *Barringtonia* seeds before the cops came.

If you are the type of person that gets distracted by the coco-plums during a bikini contest, you understand. If you visit a National Park and find yourself gathering wildflower seeds when you're supposed to be hanging up your food to keep it from the bears, you get it. If you have to put your hands in your pockets so you don't stuff cuttings into your purse when you take your children to Flamingo Gardens, this chapter is for you.

There are plants you need, with a deep and burning desire that cannot be quenched. Normal people don't understand. And the orange-vested workers in the Home Depot garden department can't speak Latin or tell you if the sad-looking pot-ted palm in the discount display is *Dypsis lutescens,* or, more tantalizingly, *Areca catechu.*

When I ran my plant nursery, I became the supplier of many hard-to-find plants. I didn't care about azaleas and mondo grass, *Dracaenas* or daylilies. No, I was the guy that supplied amaz-ing and useful niche plants, like soap-nut trees, white-fruited mulberries, edible-leafed hibiscus and black pepper vines.

Finding some of those plants often took me years, then I had to keep what I found alive as well as grow it up and propagate it. Over time, I got much better at hunting down rare plants, especially edibles. In this chapter, I'll cover how you can do the same thing.

Grocery Stores and Produce Stands

When you think of finding plants, the grocery store probably doesn't make the list. Yet it should, as the produce aisle and the dry beans section of the store can be a veritable treasure trove of planting material. Think of all the possibilities! You can grow avocado pits and garlic cloves, lentils and kidney beans, wheat berries and watermelon seeds, pomegranate seeds, mango pits, turmeric root and green onions. You can even root roses from the bouquets for sale. You can plant the seeds from dried goji berries and dates, as well as grape and lemon seeds. You can start apple, orange, lime and papaya seeds. It's ridiculous—and that's just in your normal, run-of-the-mill grocery store. The bulk dispensers at organic markets are particularly rich, providing flax seeds and mung beans, mustard and buckwheat, fava beans and rye berries. During the holidays you can get assortments of tree nuts and Indian corn. I germinated chestnuts I bought at a grocery store. The ones we didn't eat, that is.

The variety of plants available gets even more interesting when you visit ethnic markets. There can can find Nopal cactus pads—which root easily—various chayote squash, which can be planted like one huge seed, sugar cane stems that can be chopped up and planted in the garden, purple sweet potatoes, pigeon peas, mung beans, herbs and spices—there is a ton that can be grown.

Another good place to find interesting plants is at your local farmer's market. If you find a beautiful pumpkin, take it home, eat it and plant the seeds. If you get locally grown fruit, plant the seeds, as they'll make trees which are perfectly adapted to your climate. If you get to talk to the farmers at their stands, take the time to ask about what grows best in your area. Often, they'll even share seeds and plants with you. I often share produce and seeds with people and find that lots and lots of the same come back to me.

Wherever produce is sold, there is something you can grow. You just need to put your chlorophyll-colored glasses on and let the possibilities reveal themselves.

Gardening Clubs and Non-Profits

When in the Gainesville area, my wife and I volunteered for the Edible Plant Project, spending a pleasant afternoon checking out all the interesting plants and potting up rooted cuttings. The Edible Plant Project is a non-profit with a mission to:

> … *promote edible landscaping and local food abundance in North Central Florida. The goal of the EPP is to create positive alternatives to the unsustainable food system in this country. We maintain a nursery for hardy native and exotic vegetables, teas, fruit and nut trees, and a seed bank, and we share these with the community through work trade, barter, or adoption. Our plants are well suited for this gardening*

zone and easy to care for. A special focus of EPP is tree crops and various well adapted or native perennials (and some annuals) including various berries, fig, feijoa, loquat, pear, pecan, and persimmon trees and more. They make heavy crops of delicious fruit and nuts every year. These wonders of nature need to be planted only once, and they yield abundantly for decades, often with little or no care. Anyone who has ever stood under a tree loaded with fruit, gorging themselves on the crop, can appreciate the freely given abundance.[*]

Last time I was in Ft. Lauderdale, I was invited to attend a meeting of the Rare Fruit and Vegetable Council of Broward County, who are:

… dedicated to educating our members and the public about the methods for growing and propagating rare tropical fruits and vegetables and introducing the local community to new species of rare fruits and vegetables with promising nutritional values.

I visited their gardens and was amazed by the diversity of plants there. Despite some severe hurricane damage a few years back, they were still maintaining a wide range of delicious plant species.

---

[*] https://edibleplantproject.org/about/

In Lake Wales, Florida, you'll find H.E.A.R.T., a missionary training facility and non-profit which now features a nursery founded by my friend Josh Jamison. They offer:

> … *unique edible plants from around the world, specializing in perennial vegetables and fruits. We aim to provide quality plants at affordable prices as a service to the community. The plants we offer are locally adapted and well-suited for edible landscaping, permaculture and community gardening. Nursery sales help support the HEART Village educational facility which trains students to serve in poverty relief work and missions around the world.* [*]

Another great resource for plants is ECHO in Ft. Myers, which also has a very good nursery, along with a huge library of agricultural data available for farmers, non-profits, missionaries and researchers around the world:

> *ECHO is an knowledge hub for development practitioners around the world. We gather solutions from around the world that are solving hunger problems and disseminate them to our active network. These solutions promote sustainable farming techniques, nutritional plants, and appropriate technologies. They are well tested and proven to be successful over and over again.*

---

[*] https://heartvillage.org/village-nursery/

Our purpose is to help those who are teaching farmers around the world know how to be more effective in producing enough to meet the needs of their families and their communities. They in turn teach others and the ECHO effect continues!

They also carry my books in their bookstore, so you know they're legit.

And this is just in my home state of Florida. There are thousands and thousands of places like this around the world and chances are there's a great organization already in your neck of the woods. I have barely scratched the surface on the many opportunities you'll find with garden clubs, non-profits, botanical gardens and other groups. Find your local gardening groups, gardens, clubs and agricultural non-profits, get linked in and volunteering, and start collecting some amazing plants while helping others.

Meetup.com is a good resource for finding less formal local groups. In the past I have been a member of multiple gardening groups there, though I now live so far out in the jungle it is no longer useful.

Online Communities

Another option is to go online and see what's cooking in the wild and woolly world of seed trading and gardening forums. For a chance to connect with local people, beyond meeting people with Meetup.com, there are also seed-trading forums across the internet, such as https://www.reddit.com/r/seedswap/. I've also seen some good exchanging take place at Permies.com and even in the YouTube chat section of my livestreams.

There are plenty of packages traveling back-and-forth between plant collectors thanks to forums. Search for online seed exchanges and see what you can find.

Plant Shows

If you want to have a truly amazing weekend, hit a plant show. Bring all your credit cards so you can max them out buying stuff you've never seen before. It's an… investment!

Many niche nurseries set up booths at plant shows, exhibiting species you never even knew existed. I got two varieties of rare figs at one show, neither of which were *Ficus carica*. I also scored at least a dozen other plants, ranging from a nice potted coffee tree to a bushy perennial marigold. There were vendors dedicated to rare orchids, carnivorous plants, endangered native species, fruit trees and bushes, vegetables, herbs and even species of native pawpaw. Plant shows are the bread-and-butter income for quite a few small nurseries, many of which you won't find anywhere else, including online.

Look up local plant shows, and if possible, hit some of the bigger ones in nearby cities. You'll have a great time.

Mail-Order Nurseries

There are many mail order nurseries online, some of which are very good and some which are not. Burnt Ridge Nursery, Peaceful Valley Farm & Garden Supply, Grower Jim, Dave Wilson Nursery, Woodlanders and Kuffel Creek Apple Nursery are some of my favorites. My least favorites are Ty Ty Georgia and Willis Orchards. I like Gurney's catalog but have found their cheap trees to be less than impressive. I also find that the trees the Arbor Day Foundation gives away are pretty chintzy. Your mileage may vary.

For seeds, Baker Creek Heirloom Seeds is an excellent source for a great variety of rare vegetable seeds, as is the Southern Exposure Seed Exchange. On the west coast, Territorial Seed is another good one. Victory Seed Company sells tobacco seeds. I run the risk of leaving someone out by starting a list, so I'll stop here. There are plenty of great seed companies and mail order often allows you to get lots of things you won't find locally.

eBay

eBay can be great and it can be terrible. There are a lot of ridiculously stupid plant scams on there. Basically, if you find a rare plant listing from China, assume it's fraudulent. Blue watermelons, inappropriately shaped fruits, rainbow-colored orchids... it's a minefield of nonsense. I've had my garden photos stolen from my website and used by eBay scammers. I've also heard from multiple people who bought various seeds on the platform which failed to germinate or were not what was advertised. Don't be gullible. If it looks super amazing, it's probably fake. On the other hand, there are some very good vendors with backyard nurseries who use eBay as their main selling platform. My recommendation is to check out the seller reviews—and the reviewers, to make sure they're not badly-written bot-style reviews—and only buy from people in the US, UK, Canada or other less fraud-riddled society. I wish eBay would stay on top of the massive amount of foreign scammers, but it is what it is. *Caveat emptor.*

So—now that you have some good sources for weird plants, let's look at the specifics of propagating and seed saving for 101 species.

7

101 Plants and How to Propagate Them

Acerola Cherry

Also known as the Barbados cherry, the acerola cherry is a favorite of children, bearing a beautiful red fruit with a trio of small winged seeds inside. I have found them to root readily from cuttings under good conditions, so I haven't tried growing them from seed.

According to Julia F. Morton:

If seeds are used for planting, they should be selected from desirable clones not exposed to cross-pollination by inferior types. They should be cleaned, dried, and dusted with a fungicide. It should also be realized that the seeds in an individual fruit develop unevenly and only those that are fully developed when the fruit is ripe will germinate satisfac-

torily. Germination rates may be only 50% or as low as 5%. Seedlings should be transferred from flats to containers when 2 to 3 in (5–7.5 cm) high. Air-layering (in summer) and side-veneer, cleft, or modified crown grafting are feasible but not popular because it is so much easier to raise the tree from cuttings. Cuttings of branches 1/4 to 1/2 in (6–12.5 mm) thick and 8 to 10 in (20–25 cm) long, with 2 or 3 leaves attached, hormone-treated and set in sand or other suitable media under constant or intermittent mist, will root in 60 days. They are then transplanted to nursery rows or containers and held in shade for 6 months or a year before being set out in the field. Some fruits will be borne a year after planting but a good crop cannot be expected until the 3rd or 4th year. The tree will continue bearing well for about 15 years. There is a lapse of only 22 days between flowering and complete fruit maturity.[*]

I was once given some branches from a sweet-fruited variety which I used for a propagation demonstration of the mini-greenhouse bags and pots method I mentioned earlier in this book. I stuck my cuttings in soil, wet them well, then bagged the pots inside white bags from the grocery store. I set the bagged cuttings beneath a potting bench and proceeded to forget about them. While doing some garden clean up a few months later, I found multiple white, tied bags, and opened

---

[*] https://hort.purdue.edu/newcrop/morton/barbados_cherry.html

them up to see what was inside. To my surprise, they were full of rooted acerola cherry trees, happily leafing out in their grocery bag greenhouses.

Ackee

Ackee trees grow easily from fresh seeds, and can also be air-layered or started from cuttings. Seeds can take a couple of months to sprout and likely need to be harvested fresh and planted before they desiccate. The downside of growing from seed is that seedling ackee trees can take six or more years to fruit and the fruit is of variable quality. Air-layered or grafted trees will bear faster, as will trees started from cuttings. Still, I am a fan of seedling trees and would happily mow around any well-placed seedling that showed up on my land.

Aloe

Aloes are very easy to propagate. All you need to do is divide off the pups and plant them out. Leaves will just rot if planted. Don't overwater your aloes, as they are adapted to arid climates.

Almond

Crack open the almond shell and remove the kernel, soak it in water for a few hours, plant it in some slightly moist potting soil in a Ziploc bag, then pop the bag in your fridge. A few months later, the almond should start developing roots. At this point, plant the kernel in a pot. When the plant is ready, it will emerge and start making leaves. If you feel more adventurous, you can just plant almonds outdoors in fall in pots or in the ground and let the winter weather stratify them. Just don't forget where you planted your seeds.

I have heard that the "raw almonds" sold in the US are actually heat-treated and unviable, so you may have to find an almond tree to get truly raw seeds, or purchase almonds that have been imported. Stick to almonds in the shell, as well, as shelled almonds may have dried out too much to be viable.

Amaranth

Amaranth is very easy to grow from seeds. You can be precise and plant the seeds in rows, carefully placing each tiny grain a couple of inches from the next, or you can plant amaranth the Good Gardener way and just scatter a few pinches over a prepared seed bed and crumble them into the ground, then water them in. Seeds usually germinate in a week or so in warm weather. Amaranth doesn't like freezing, so be sure you plant late enough in the spring that your plants won't get killed by a frost. Let some of the plants go to bloom. When they're full of seeds, you can rub the blooms together between your hands and the seeds will fall out. Save them for your next garden. Amaranth is also good at re-seeding, so you may not even have to replant.

Apple

All you need to do is eat a few apples and save the seeds. Do not dry them out. I stratify them in the fridge using the moist soil and Ziploc bag method described for almonds. Once you see little roots and shoots, transplant your apple seedling.

Occasionally, apple seeds will already be germinating inside the apple or will start right away from the fruit. My friend Steven Edholm of the Skillcult blog, remarked on one of my apple propagation videos that many apples are stored under refrigeration which breaks the dormancy cycle of the seeds, so sometimes all you need to sprout apple seeds is to plant them directly.

Don't place your newly transplanted apple seedlings right into full sun. Find a shady spot and put them there and take extra care when they're young. Seedling apples are very prone to rotting, so don't overwater them. Soon they'll be large enough transplant into your orchard or food forest. Seedling apples also make good rootstocks for grafting.

Apricot

Germinate as you would almonds.

Arrowroot

Arrowroot can be started from roots, dug, divided and re-planted wherever you want to grow arrowroot. It's an attractive plant that fits well into edible landscaping.

When you're growing arrowroot and it starts to die in the fall, don't fear. It's just going into dormancy. On my old North Florida homestead they would freeze to the ground in winter and come back again in the spring, much like ginger. That's the time I pull the roots. Give them a year of growth and they'll usually make at least a half-dozen or more harvestable roots. Give them two years and you'll get a lot more than that. In the tropics, they die back in the dry season and reemerge with the rains.

Avocado

Though you are probably familiar with the "toothpicks and water" method of sprouting avocado pits, there is an easier way.

The short of it? Plant them in dirt, as God intended!

Avocados, like many tropical trees, have seeds that are designed to hit the ground and grow. The pits are not designed like many cold-climate seeds which have an embryo sitting in suspended animation that can be saved on a shelf for a long time and then spring to life when planted.

These guys need to get into the ground fast, so it's important to plant your avocados quickly or keep them damp until you can plant.

Open an avocado and take out the pit, then plant the pit in soil. You don't have to plant them deep. They'll come up if they're only half-planted in soil and they'll come up if they're buried a few inches down. I usually plant them just below the surface.

A nice, loose potting mix is good but you can also easily germinate avocado pits directly planted in the ground—or, what seems to be even more successful, let them "accidentally" come up in your compost pile and transplant them.

The hard part is waiting for the avocado pits to sprout. Just keep them watered but not soggy in a nice sunny location, and in a month or two, they'll send up a vigorous shoot.

When you sprout pits in water indoors, they then need to go through a "hardening off" period of adjustment to the harsher, brighter outdoor conditions or you can kill the young trees. When you instead sprout them in pots in full sun, you don't have this issue. They're ready to go. The earliest a seedling avocado tree will fruit is at four to five years of age. I once had multiple avocados show up in my yard because I had buried compost here and there in melon pits I'd planted over with watermelons. Despite being buried deeply, the avocado pits that came through with the other kitchen waste managed to germinate and grow. Of course, I let them.

The California Avocado Commission[*] claims it takes 5–13 years for a seedling tree to bear, but you're much more likely to see it fruit on the earlier end of that spectrum if they are well-tended, watered and grown in full sun.

---

[*] http://www.californiaavocado.com/how-tos/your-own-avocado-tree

If you want faster avocados, graft a scion from a mature tree onto your seedling, then you can get fruit in as little as a couple of years. Reports on growing avocados from cuttings and air layering are mixed, with Mexican cuttings perhaps performing better[*] than non-Mexican types. Mexican avocado genetics can be determined by crushing a leaf and smelling it. If it smells like anise, you have a Mexican type.

My recommendation for faster fruiting: start a bunch of pits, then practice your grafting. I also recommend you plant a few trees around your yard to ensure pollination. Or plant three trees in the same hole.

Banana

Most of us know that modern bananas are seedless. They weren't that way originally, but over time the seeds were bred out of them, most likely under the tutelage of the Watchers.

We now propagate most banana plants with cloning methods, such as dividing off the pups or with tissue culture. Clones are not good for genetic diversity, but they are good for getting consistent results.

Divide off small, healthy pups and plant them out. You can also dig up a big clump of banana trees, cut the stalks off, divide off all the bulbs and plant them.

Some years ago I learned about a more in depth method from ECHO which allows you to create many dozens of plants from

---

[*] https://www.researchgate.net/publication/268432764_Rooting_Avocado_Cuttings

a single banana bulb. It's a rather complicated procedure, but if you are interested in pursuing it, you will find instructions online by searching for the article "Rapid Multiplication of Banana and Plantain Plants" by Darren Boss.

Basil

Basil grows readily from seeds, which usually germinate in a couple of weeks. To save seeds, let your basil plants go to seed. When the blooms have dried brown, tip out the tiny black seeds. There is a sterile perennial form of basil, known as African blue basil, which is very attractive to pollinators. That one starts readily from cuttings.

Bean

Beans are one of the first plants I grew. Plant about a half to one inch deep in warm soil after all danger of frost and they usually pop up in a week or less. Some varieties of beans have harder shells. With those, you can nick them first and soak overnight so they swell up, then plant. If they don't swell up in water overnight, you didn't give them a good enough nick. Try again, and soak again, then plant.

Save bean pods after they have dried brown on the plant, then crack them open to get your beans. Some pods, like those of the velvet bean, shatter open when dry.

Beet

Beet seeds are actually a dried fruit with multiple seeds inside. Plant them a half-inch deep and a couple of inches apart and they'll pop up within a couple weeks. Beets are a bit poky at the beginning, taking their sweet time to emerge.

Though I have not grown beets for seed, the Center for Food Safety seed-saving list recommends the following practices:

> *In fall, identify the beets that you would like to use for seed. Once the tops have begun to yellow and flop over, tie the stalks to stakes for support. Look for flowers in early summer (June or July). ... When the seed spikes are dry on the plant (they will turn a brown/tan color), cut them and place them in a paper bag to dry for two additional weeks. Once seeds are completely dry, rub the seed spikes to separate the seeds. ... Store in a cool, dry place. Beet seeds can last up to four years. ... Beets are biennial, so only produce seed in the second year after sowing. This poses a challenge for seed savers in cold climates. Beets should be able to survive the winter in climates with average annual minimum temperatures of -10 degrees F or warmer. If you live in a colder climate, we recommend storing the beets through the winter and replanting in the spring.*[*]

---

[*] https://www.globalseednetwork.org/seed-tips-detail.php?id=5

Bilimbi

Bilimbi grows readily from seed. Pick ripe fruit and take out the seeds. I scrub off the pulp, wash them, then plant in pots. Germination takes about a month. Air-layering is reportedly not worthwhile.

Blueberry

Blueberry cuttings root in a few months under mist or using the mini-greenhouse method. I have started them on my windowsill without trouble. You can also start them from seeds but that seems like an unnecessary pain to me, considering how tiny the seeds are.

Breadfruit

Chop through some of the roots around an established tree and suckers should appear, which you can then dig and pot up. Keep watered well as they establish. You can also start breadfruit via root cuttings. The Food and Agriculture Organization of the United Nations has a pdf on the topic sharing the process:

> *The use of root cuttings is the most suitable method that is currently available for commercial production of young breadfruit plants. Root cuttings can be used to produce young breadfruit plants because they can be induced to produce adventitious shoots. Many nurseries use one root cutting to*

produce one plant but this is wasteful and can weaken the stock plants from which they are taken if roots cuttings are collected from the same trees annually. Instead, one cutting can be used to produce many shoots. … The propagating bin should be located under 50% shade and with a clean, well-drained medium such as river sand to a depth of at least 20 cm (8").

Materials:

- *Black plastic bags (15 cm x 30 or 35 cm)*

- *Soil mixture or growing medium—This should consist of a mixture of soil, organic matter and sharp sand in suitable proportions, for example, 3:2:1 or 2:1:1, to allow for proper drainage with good moisture retention.*

Tools: – *Lopper or bow saw – Secateurs or sharp knife*

Procedures:

1. *Cut pieces of root, at least 1m (3') long with a diameter of 5 to 7 cm (2" to 3") wide, from roots growing close to the surface. Before lifting the piece of root or root cutting, place a notch at one end to mark the upper surface of the root.*

2. Immediately after lifting the cutting, dip both ends in a 6% potassium permanganate solution and also brush some of the solution on the cut end of the root in the soil. This treatment coagulates and stops the flow of latex and sap out of the cuttings.

3. Wash the root cuttings free of soil. Use a soft brush to dislodge any soil that is not easily removed by water. The cuttings should be brushed gently to avoid damage to their surface. Do not soak the cuttings in water for long periods.

4. Cut them into smaller pieces, 30 to 60 cm (1' to 2') long, that can be accommodated in a propagating bin. Remember to notch the upper surface at one end of the cutting. Additionally, 2 to 4 cuts, just about 2 to 3 mm (1/8") deep may be made with a clean, sharp knife along the length of the cutting to encourage multiple shoot development.

5. Place the cuttings horizontally in the bin with the notched surface of the root uppermost as it was in the soil and cover with a 1 cm (0.5") layer of sand.

6. *This layer of sand should be kept moist, but not wet, preferably by an overhead misting system. If a misting system is not available, the sand should be kept moist by watering using a hose or can with a fine holes in the head or spout to minimize removing the sand, and by covering the bin with plastic to maintain high humidity. However, avoid over-watering as this encourages root rot. Apply fungicides taking care to rotate them. Within 4 to 6 weeks, adventitious shoots should begin to appear.*

7. *Cut the shoots after several leaves have developed and the stems are elongated and hardened in the lower portion as shown by its brown color. Use clean secateurs or a clean, sharp knife to remove only the upper portion of the shoot. Place the cut at the semi-hard (greenish brown) portion of the stem and at least 2.5 cm (1") below a node. Be careful to leave the lower nodes intact because from these additional shoots will arise and should be harvested in a similar manner.*

8. *Dip the cut ends of the shoot cuttings in rooting powder for semi-hard shoots or in an auxin*

solution with an appropriate concentration to increase the root number.

9. *Place the cut shoots to root in another shaded (50%) bin in damp sand, under mist or very high relative humidity conditions. Rooting takes place in 3–4 weeks.*

10. *The rooted cuttings are then potted in plastic bags containing a suitable rooting medium. Apply water and maintain the young plants under shade and high humidity for about 2 weeks. Do not space the plant too closely in the nursery since this increases shade and will encourage rapid vertical shoot growth which can be a disadvantage in the field. Harden them gradually by reducing shade. Note that the medium should be kept moist but not wet and during this period, a complete fertilizer with a high P ratio should be applied. Pesticides should only be used if required. The plants are ready for field planting in 5 to 6 months.*[*]

Breadfruit can also be air-layered, or breadnut seeds can be planted, then breadfruit scions can be grafted on to the resultant seedlings.

---

[*] http://www.fao.org/3/a-i3085e.pdf

Broccoli

Broccoli is easy to grow from seed.

When you harvest broccoli, just cut the first big head off before it starts to spread open and the yellow blooms appear. Then keep checking on the plant… it's going to grow multiple side shoots that will make many smaller heads as they grow. You can let these go to seed, then save the seeds.

In my experience, broccoli does best right from seed, rather than as a transplant. Of course, most plants do. Forget the expensive transplants—buy a pack of seeds and scatter away, then thin them out and eat the thinnings.

Canna Lily

To propagate, just chop into a clump and divide off what you want, then plant out elsewhere. The rhizotamaceous (yeah, I think I made that word up) roots will make a big mat over time. Harvest as you like and plant what you don't eat.

If you want to start them from seeds, look for the weird tri-lobed spiky seed pods that appear after the flowers fade. As they dry, the sides will split and reveal black or brown seeds that are about the size of buckshot. These seeds are REALLY hard and can apparently remain viable for centuries. They're supposed to be hard to start, but they're not, provided you do it right. Take a pair of nail clippers or a little file and make nips in the sides of the seeds. They're white inside—if you get to the white, you're doing fine. Then soak those suckers in water for a day or two. They'll swell up if you went deep enough with your nicking. This is a bit tough to do, since the seed coats are really hard. The soaked seeds germinate about a week or two after planting. Growth is rapid and the baby plants can be planted out in a month or two. I had a ton of them at my old property, since a gal at the local ag extension dumped a bunch of seeds on me since they're "too hard for people to start and we don't think we can sell them on our seed rack." Challenge accepted.

Cane Fruit

Blackberries and raspberries can be propagated by cuttings and by tip layering. With cuttings, cut canes into 3–6" pieces, dip in rooting hormone, then put under mist or in mini-greenhouses. You can also use root cuttings. Cut roughly 1/4" thick roots off near the parent plant, dividing into roughly 6" segments. The part of the root that was nearest the mother plant will produce the growing buds, so plant your root cuttings with that side near the surface of the soil. Seeds can be cleaned, scarified, then stratified for 3–4 months in the fridge, then planted in soil. You can also divide plants with a shovel and plant out. Cane fruit are easy to propagate.

Carob

I germinated carob seeds easily with the nick, soak, and plant method. They came up readily; however, the roots on carob are very long and they do not transplant well. I recommend either starting them in deep pots or planting directly in the ground.

According to the New Agriculturalist:

> *Planting stock is usually raised in nurseries from seeds although, if planting carob on land previously used for agriculture, stands can be created by direct sowing. Planting stock can also be propagated by cuttings, suckers, layers and air-layering. For fast growing and high yielding trees, buds from good varieties are grafted to 3–4 year old seedlings in the field. As a dioecious species (separate male and female plants), female trees need to be inter-spaced with 5% well-placed male trees, which provide the necessary pollen. Only the female trees produce brown leathery pods (up to 1 foot long) 11 months after pollination. Density of established trees can range from 25 to 100 plants per hectare.*[*]

Carob is a good alternative to chocolate in drier and cooler climates.

Carrot

Carrots are a pain to germinate as they like to be shallowly sowed and consistently moist, plus they take 2–3 weeks to come up. Herrick Kimball has eased the pain of carrot germination,

---

[*] http://www.new-ag.info/00-2/focuson/focuson5.html

however, and you can see a video series he did on YouTube by searching for "Four-Day Carrots".

Saving your own carrot seed isn't hard, though you have to watch out because carrots happily breed with wild Queen Anne's lace plants. Carrots go to seed in their second year of growth. If your garden temperatures go below the mid-teens, you'll have to dig your carrot roots and stick them in the fridge for the winter, then re-plant the roots in the spring so they can go to seed.

Cashew

Germinating cashew nuts is easy, provided you have fresh, raw cashew seeds at the onset.

If you live in the tropics where cashews grow, getting fresh cashews for germination is just a matter of picking seeds up off the ground. However, I can confidently assert that this isn't the case for most of you, so the biggest trick to growing a cashew from seed is actually finding a seed to grow. First, don't buy a bag of cashews and plant them. That would be an expensive waste of tasty nuts. Even if they are "raw", they are long-dead.

The cashew nuts you plant need to be raw, unshelled—and quite fresh!

According to The World Agroforestry Centre:

Seed storage behavior is orthodox; 100% germination has been recorded after 4 months of open storage at room tem-

*perature, but viability is reduced to 50% after 10 months
and none survives after 13–14 months.*[*]

A few years ago when I lived in Florida an Asian friend/fan
smuggled in a fresh cashew from the tropics and gave it to me
at the farmer's market.

"How did you get this?" I asked.

"You need to hide seeds inside your bag of dirty underwear!"
she said. "They never check there!"

I have really hardcore fans.

Unfortunately, that seed failed to germinate (it probably died
of embarrassment) so I was stuck cashew-less until I bought a
tree from Spyke's Grove Farm and Nursery and added it The
Great South Florida Food Forest Project the next year.

If you're able to find fresh cashew seeds, plant them right
away a couple of inches deep during warm weather. They grow
quite quickly and bear young.

Cassava

Unlike many plants, cassava is not usually grown from seeds
except for breeding purposes. The only way most folks grow
it is via stem cuttings. Roots from the grocery store almost
definitely won't work since they've been separated from the stem
and dipped in wax.

---

[*] http://www.worldagroforestry.org/treedb2/speciesprofile.php?Spid=205

To grow from fresh cuttings, chop woody stems into pieces about 1.5' long, stick them in the ground on their sides about two inches down and cover them lightly with soil—or, as I plant them, stuck in vertically with the growth buds pointing up—and, if the weather is warm, within a week or so they will start growing new leaves.

Celosia

Propagate like amaranth. I grow *Celosia argentea* as a leaf vegetable and it regularly self-seeds.

Chaya / Mexican Tree Spinach

Cuttings root in a month or so when it's warm. Just cut some cuttings, remove the leaves, let the sap at the wound dry, stick them in somewhat moist soil and wait. They're not as fast as their cousin cassava but they'll usually take. Chaya stems are waxy and can be often left laying around in the shade for months before planting and they'll still grow.

Cherry

Clean fruit off pits, plant in slightly moist soil in a Ziploc bag, stratify for at least three months, then plant.

Chinese Water Chestnut

Chinese water chestnut is a sedge that produces edible corms. I used to grow them in a bathtub. They like a few inches of water and some muck to root into. If you can get a fresh Chinese water chestnut root, pop it into some wet muck and it will usually start growing within a couple of weeks. I've found Chinese water chestnuts also reproduce well by division. Just pull a clump of reeds out of your bathtub with some roots on the bottom and plant them into another bathtub of muck and water. Easy!

Chinese Yam

Chinese yam (*Dioscorea batatas* aka *Dioscorea polystachya*) produces a very good root and can be grown all the way up to USDA zone 4, unlike its other cousins in the good ol' *Dioscorea spp*. Eric Toensmeier calls this species the "yamberry" because of the small and prolific crops of edible bulbils produced on the vines. We're not going to talk about eating them in this book, obviously—no, we need to grow them. Stop! If you eat them, you won't have anything to plant! The bulbils form in late summer and fall. Harvest them when the vines die back in late fall and winter. Unlike *Dioscorea alata* and *Dioscorea bulbifera*, which both have large aerial tubers you can plant, the small bulbils on Chinese yam are a little harder to manage and grow. In my experience, if you leave them out on a counter through the winter months they're just going to dry out and they won't be worth planting. Instead, I recommend planting them shallowly in some slightly moist soil until they emerge in the spring. You might also be able keep them viable in some sawdust. When the vines start growing, plant them out in the garden after all danger of frost. There is a good chance you can also propagate this species by dividing the large roots the yam produces beneath the ground; however, they are quite delicate and I haven't been able to try it myself or find data.

Chocolate Pudding Fruit

Like many tropical trees without real winter dormancy periods, the seed germination rate of chocolate pudding fruit, aka black sapote, declines rapidly in storage. Fresh is best. They need to be planted right away, if possible, for good success.

I've planted some seeds that were a few months old and they didn't grow at all. On my porch I have some I took from fresh fruits and planted a few days later. They are coming up less than a month after planting.

According to the University of Florida:

Black sapote may be propagated by seed, marcottage (air-layering, budding, and grafting. Black sapote varieties do not come true from seed and seedling trees may take up to 5 or 6 years to flower. Trees with only male flowers will not produce fruit; trees with female or male and female flowers *will bear fruit. Superior fruit varieties and selections are therefore propagated by budding and grafting.*[*]

I hadn't heard previously of there being some trees that are solely male; however, this is the case with their cousin the American persimmon. If you grow a tree and have that kind of poor luck, graft on some female scion wood and leave one male branch for pollinating the rest. The tree I have growing in South Florida is self-fertile, which was likely a trait selected by nurserymen.

The Rare Fruit Club of Australia covers the issue in short:

Black sapote is usually andromonecious, i.e., it has both male and hermaphrodite flowers on the same tree. The axillary flowers are normally solitary if hermaphrodite and in clusters of 3–7 if male. They are white and tubular-lobed with a persistent 4-lobed green calyx and an ovary with 8–12 carpels. Self-incompatibility has been reported for some isolated trees; others may produce only male flowers. Pollination is by insects.[†]

Since many gardeners grow black sapote from seed and it's the most common means of propagation, it sounds like the "male only" thing is an uncommon problem. Plant away—just plant fresh seeds.

---

[*] http://edis.ifas.ufl.edu/hs305
[†] http://www.rarefruitclub.org.au/Level2/BlackSapote.htm

Cilantro

Seed directly into the ground, a quarter to half-inch deep, after all danger of frost. In North Florida, my cilantro self-seeded regularly and returned on its own for multiple years in a row.

Citrus

Just this morning I went outside and was pleased to see the calamondin and kumquat seeds I planted two weeks ago are happily germinating on my porch. To germinate citrus seeds, get seeds from a fresh fruit, then wash and plant them. If you let the seeds dry on your counter for a few months, they'll die. Just use fresh seed. A few weeks on the counter may be okay, but a few months will doom your trees. Smaller citrus, like key lime, kumquats and lemons, often bear in just a few years, whereas oranges and grapefruit reportedly take as long as 8–10 years to bear from seed.

Coconut

In order to get a coconut to germinate, you need to first start with a mature nut that has milk inside.

Once you plant that, it's just a matter of waiting. You can even grow them indoors if you aren't in the tropics. As the University of Hawaii directs:

> To grow a coconut palm as a house plant, use a container at
> least 10 inches deep and large enough in diameter to hold the

nut. Use a well drained potting soil mix. After soaking the nut, plant it with the pointed end down and the end that was attached to the tree upward. About a third of the nut should be above the soil level. Water it frequently, keeping the soil moist but not wet. As long as the soil drains well, it is difficult to give the germinating nut too much water. Keep the container in a warm location, preferably where the temperature never falls below 70°F and often is above 80°F. A container specimen should grow to be around 5 ft high and survive in the same container for about five years.

To grow the coconut in your yard, choose a site with well drained soil in partial shade. Place the nut on its side in a shallow hole, burying only the lower third of the nut. Water it thoroughly twice a week.

Under ideal conditions, a coconut will germinate in three months, but otherwise it may take up to six months. At germination, the roots should push out through the husk, and the first shoot, looking like a sharp green spear, will emerge from the cavity at the end of the nut that was attached to the tree.

All you need to do is just bury a coconut part way and keep it watered. If it's viable, it will grow.

My grandpop used to stuff coconuts into the holes the land crabs would make in his backyard in an attempt to slow down their assault on his St. Augustine grass. Eventually, some of them would germinate and he'd have to pull them out before they got too big. I transplanted one into my parents' backyard when I was 15 and it's now a big, beautiful tree, loaded with fruit.

You can often find baby coconuts sprouting in untended areas around coconut palms where the nuts have simply come to rest on the soil. They transplant readily and will happily grow even in clay soils, provided they don't ever freeze.

In Florida coconuts usually fruit 6–8 years after sprouting. In the tropics I have been told that a happy tree can fruit in as little as four years.

Cocoa

According to the International Cocoa Organization:

Cocoa is raised from seed. Seeds will germinate and produce good plants when taken from pods not more than 15 days underripe.

Vegetative propagation can also be used to create clones. Vegetative propagation can be by cuttings, budding or marcotting.

Cuttings—Tree cuttings are taken with between two and five leaves and one or two buds. The leaves are cut in half and the cutting placed in a pot under polythene until roots begin to grow.

Budding—*A bud is cut from a tree and placed under a flap of bark on another tree. The budding patch is then bound with raffia, waxed tape of clear plastic to prevent moisture loss. When the bud is growing the old tree above it is cut down.*

Marcotting—*A strip of bark is removed from a branch and the area covered in sawdust and a polythene sheet. The area will produce roots and the branch can then be chopped off and planted.*[*]

I have grown cocoa from seed accidentally. My children and I sucked the fruit off the seeds and spit them into the compost, where they later germinated. Cocoa takes a week or more to sprout and you will often find seeds germinating inside overripe pods. One thing you can't do is grow cocoa from dry nibs—they're dead. Get very fresh seed and plant it right out of the fruit.

From seed, cocoa usually begins fruiting in 3–5 years.

Coffee

Here's why germinating coffee seeds is a little tough:

1. You need fresh seeds

I've bought coffee seeds through the mail and tried to germinate them. They all failed. If the seeds are more than a few weeks—

---

[*] https://www.icco.org/faq/48-biotechnology/112-propagation-of-cocoa-trees.html

or maybe months—old, they may not come up. Roasted beans from the store are obviously not going to work, so finding green, non-aged seeds is the first thing you need to do to get started. I paid $30 for my mother coffee tree and then waited a year for seeds so I could get started on my future plantation.

2. It takes time for coffee to germinate

Coffee beans usually take a couple of months to germinate. Even then, the germination is uneven and hasn't been that high. Maybe 50%. Bottom heat helps. I've had them come up in a month with a heating pad (like this one) beneath my seed trays. You need to keep them moist during this time. I put the seed trays on a large oven sheet with a little water in the bottom so they don't dry out. That works well for me.

3. It takes time for coffee to grow

From germination, it takes 2–3 years for your new coffee tree to start fruiting. Fortunately, coffee is self-pollinating so you'll be able to get beans off a tree without its needing a mate. The plants I sold were mostly about 6 months old and 6–8" tall. They grow moderately quickly if you keep them in acidic soil and supplied with nitrogen. I feed mine with rabbit manure and coffee grounds. Blood meal is another good choice.

Collards

To plant the easy way, prepare a bare patch of ground, then scatter seeds, rake them around, and water for a week. Baby plants will come up everywhere. Thin as needed to give them space for growth and eat the thinnings. Harvest leaves as needed—the plants will take a lot of cutting.

Collards are a biennial and will bloom in the second year, so if you have very harsh winters you'll need to dig the plants in fall and overwinter them in a root cellar or outbuilding, then re-plant in the spring so they can bloom. Save seeds when pods are dry and hard.

Corn

Plant corn directly in the ground, up to 3" deep, where you want it to grow. Corn is often sold as transplants, but that is ridiculous. It does way better sown directly in the ground. To save seeds, wait for the ears to dry on the plants, bring them inside and let them dry more on the cob, then crack off the kernels and store in the fridge until next season.

Cucumber

Did you ever miss harvesting a cucumber then find out that it had blown up into a huge yellow zeppelin on the vine? That's what you want for seed. Let them get big and almost rotten, then harvest the seeds. Wash and dry. Plant cucumber seeds at least a half-inch deep in the ground in nice, fertile soil after all danger of frost and give them something good to climb. Germination takes about a week.

Date

I bought some dried California dates from the supermarket for my children and told them to save the pits so I could plant them. Unfortunately, starting date palms from seed is slightly tricky. There's a lot of strange info online involving various tricks for starting palm seeds, but the following method worked for me. First I scrubbed the flesh off the date pits, then let them dry for a few days. After that, I soaked them in water for a couple of days, changing the water frequently so they didn't rot. Then I planted them a couple inches deep in a terracotta pot of moist vermiculite and set that on top of the water heater.

A couple months later after not seeing any leaves emerge, I dug into the vermiculite and discovered a few of the seeds had developed roots. I took those out and put them in pots outside to continue growing. I had sporadic germinations occur on top of the water heater for another month or so, and I potted those out as well. After a few weeks outside, they'd poke up leaves and it was off to the races. Overall, I'd say I had a germination rate of maybe 25%.

This morning, however, I woke to find that five date pits I had planted in a bag of soil on my porch had all germinated despite no special treatment. Perhaps my current tropical climate helped, but it was quite a surprise to get 100% germination rate—and all on the same day.

Dates can take 4–8 years to start fruiting from seed.

Dragon fruit

Cuttings are the easiest way to propagate dragon fruit and is the way I've done it, however Tradewinds Fruit writes the following on germinating dragon fruit seeds:

> *Dragon fruit seeds are usually fairly easy to germinate but show variable germination rates. Fresh (undried) seeds will germinate quite rapidly, usually within just a few days. Dried seeds show longer germination periods and often germinate within 1–4 weeks, though some groups may need up to 8 weeks for germination. Plant seeds 1/4–1/2" deep in moist, sterile soil. Keep soil temperature consistent at 70–85F. Cool soils will significantly delay seed germination time and may inhibit germination completely.*

> *Dragon fruit seeds are small and very fragile, so handle with care. Also take care in watering not to jostle the soil as seeds can become deeply buried where they may fail to breach the soil surface and rot.*

From cuttings, dragon fruit can bear in as little as a year. I have read it can take half a decade or more to fruit from seed.

Though I haven't done anything with the seeds, GreenGardenGuy1 on YouTube answered a comment on dragon fruit seed germination with the following:

> *It depends a lot on the variety and the growing conditions. Under the local Hawaiian conditions the Yellow dragon fruit can start producing in around 2 years from seeds. The Pink types take 5 or 6 here. I have an 8 year old red here from a cutting and it has never made a flower.*[*]

Elephant Ear

Dig and divide clumps, plant roots or portions of roots.

Enterolobium

Enterolobium cyclocarpum and *Enterolobium contortisiliquum* are both beautiful, massive rainforest trees with a remarkable ability to fix nitrogen and create biomass. I learned about their usefulness from my friend Craig Hepworth, though I had seen the weird "earpods" as a kid and marveled at them. This is a very good food forest species for chop-and-drop, though it likely isn't hardier than zone 8. In zone 8/9, it will freeze back in winter, then return again from lover on the trunk or below the ground.

To propagate, break open a pod (carefully, so as not to destroy the seeds inside), then extract the seeds, nick them, soak overnight, then plant.

[*] https://www.youtube.com/watch?v=cmRTM4ZWquE

Fig

Figs graft easily and can also be started effectively with cuttings. Use newer wood, taking foot-long (or so) cuttings. Dip ends in rooting hormone, put in a pot in the shade and water occasionally. Figs can fruit within a year from cuttings but usually take a couple of years.

Flamboyant Tree

Save seeds from mature, brown pods that rattle nicely. Nick the seeds and soak overnight, then plant. Trees grow quite rapidly.

Goumi Berry

I have propagated these in a mist house from cuttings, though the strike rate was not very good. Seeds require cold stratification before planting.

Ginger

Divide roots in fall, winter and spring, then plant 2–4" deep in loose soil, ensuring there is at least one or two good "eyes" on the rhizome. Divide entire plants during the growing season and plant out.

Grape

Cuttings or ground layering work very well on grapes. I used to give away rooted portions of grape vine in the spring, as I would discover them around my vineyard where vines had touched the ground and grown roots.

Hibiscus

Some hibiscus are sterile and do not produce seed. The ones that do are usually easy to sprout. Fortunately, hibiscus species start readily from cuttings.

Hickory

Remove outer husks and plant unshelled nuts in the ground a couple of inches deep in fall wherever you want trees to grow. I usually plant a few seeds at the same time when I direct seed tree seeds, then select out the healthiest after they germinate and cut down the rest. My children inadvertently planted hickory trees across my old food forest by throwing and whacking the nuts with a baseball bat. Interestingly, pecan can be grafted onto hickory, so if you have a hickory seedling you can tack on a pecan scion.

Jackfruit

Germinating jackfruit seeds isn't hard but you do need to start with fresh seed as the seeds dry out and die quickly. You'll have to find for an ethnic market to obtain jackfruit unless you're lucky enough to live someplace where jackfruit are regularly grown.

After you're done munching on delicious jackfruit and cleaning the latex off everything in the kitchen, it's time to plant the jackfruit seeds.

Jackfruit seeds look like fat beans. If you don't have time to plant them right away, just set them aside on the counter—they'll keep for a few days.

Just don't put them in the fridge, as that might kill them. Jackfruit have very little tolerance for cold. If you need to keep them for a week or more, put the seeds in some moist soil or with a damp paper towel. They may rot or sprout if you leave them for too long, so it's better to plant quickly.

You can plant jackfruit seeds in pots, but direct-seeding jackfruit also works quite well.

If you use pots, make sure you pick deeper ones. Jackfruit like to send roots down fast and deep and will rapidly outgrow a small pot.

The first time I planted jackfruit right in the ground, I planted a half-dozen seeds and kept them watered. A month or so later, they started coming up. After a few weeks, I thinned the cluster of sprouts down to a couple of trees, then down to one a few months later. At a year of age, the tree was about 3' tall.

Plant your seeds 2" deep and wait. It will take a month or two for them to come up. Be patient and keep them watered. Before planting, I often soak seeds in water overnight in case they've dried out a bit. It seems to help.

Jackfruit come up with long, thin green shoots that resolve into two little leaves at the top.

Remember: jackfruit do much better in the ground than they

do in pots. Get them in the ground once they're a decent size and get them growing with lots of compost.

Some sites will say it takes years and years for a jackfruit to bear from seed but this isn't necessarily correct. The tree at the farm I used to rent started bearing at about 5 years of age. Your mileage may vary. Nursery owner Pete Kanaris had a seedling jackfruit bloom at only 18 months of age.

Jackfruit grow quickly and like water, fertile soil and plenty of sun. Light frosts may kill young trees but older trees can take some cold.

Jerusalem Artichoke

The plants die back in fall/winter and you can dig the huge clusters of roots that grow around the base of the stem. Plant entire tubers during the fall, winter and spring where you want more Jerusalem artichokes. I planted a bunch of them in poor ground in Tennessee and they thrived on neglect.

Kale

Let your kale go to seed and harvest when the pods are dry. Plant a quarter to half-inch deep in garden soil sometime around your last expected spring frost date or in the fall.

Lettuce

I like to scatter lettuce seeds of different varieties across a garden bed and rake them in, often mixing them with radishes, kale, spinach and other greens. Let your lettuce go to seed and shake the tiny seeds out for next year. Store in the fridge until planting time.

Leucana leucocephala

Leucana is a very useful tropical fodder crop and nitrogen fixer, also known as "false tamarind" and "lead tree". Let the pods dry brown on the tree, then save the seeds. To germinate, nick and soak the seeds over night, then plant out in pots or in the ground. The trees produce seed abundantly and have a tendency to become invasive, which makes them very good for feeding goats and using for biomass production and nitrogen fixation in a young food forest.

Loofah

Plant near a fence, about an inch deep. Germination takes 5–10 days. In tropical climates, loofahs self-seed prolifically and like semi-open woods near rivers and creeks.

Loquat

I like loquats so much I made them part of the logo for my old plant nursery. They are a pleasant sweet-tart relative of apples, plums and peaches, though they are much more perishable and have never really taken off in North American groceries. Loquats are subtropical, with the ability to take temperatures below freezing (though probably not colder than a few degrees Fahrenheit) and sail through. Unfortunately, their blooms cannot take temperatures below the mid-20s without damage, and loquats have the irritating habit of blooming in February, then having their blooms freeze off. If you want fruit, you need to protect the blooms during frost events.

There are improved varieties but even seedlings bear usable fruit. Inside each fruit is one or more soft, rounded pits. Seedling varieties often have much larger pits than improved selections. Improved varieties are also much sweeter with more flesh than seedlings.

Loquat pits must be fresh to be viable. They do not have a hard seed coat and will die if they dry out. Plant them an inch or two deep and keep them watered and they'll come up in a month or two.

I have never had luck starting loquats from cuttings; however, I visited Grandiflora Nursery in Gainesville and was amazed to see them propagating loquats from cuttings. In my own nursery, I would dig a small bed right in the ground and bury rows of loquat pits, then come back and dig up the seedlings a few months later and plant them in pots. When they reached a couple of feet in height, I would side-veneer graft on improved scion wood.

If you grow a seedling loquat from an improved tree, chances are you'll get better fruit than just planting the pits from a so-so tree growing in a landscape. Someone from the Edible Plant

Project in Gainesville collected seeds from a plant nursery that had lots of named cultivars. In that case, they knew every parent was making great fruit so the offspring would be likely to do the same.

From seed it takes about six years before you get fruit.

Mahogany

My Grandpa used to start mahogany seeds in pots on a regular basis, though I have not tried it myself.

According to cites.org:

A single fruit contains up to 60 large, winged seeds, but on average only 35–45 of these will germinate. Fruit size may vary considerably, both within a tree's crown and among different trees. Larger fruit produce larger seeds that are more likely to germinate and will produce larger seedlings. Even though most seeds fly less than 100 m from the parent tree, they are difficult to collect on the ground once dispersed, and they quickly lose the ability to germinate once exposed to the elements. The seeds are best collected from the crown, before the fruit capsule bursts open, by using proper tree-climbing equipment and an extendable pruning pole to sever the fruit where it attaches to the tree's smallest branches. The larger branches should not be cut just to bring down a few fruit— this will reduce fruit production in years to come … Ma-hogany seeds will germinate within 2–4 weeks once they have been watered. Break off the wings and plant the seeds tip down in well-draining soil (for example, sandy soil), nearly but not quite buried. In the nursery, use black polyvinyl planting bags 10–12 cm in diameter by 30 cm deep to allow the seedling to root deeply. It's best to try to use the same kind of soil in the nursery that the seedling will encounter in the forest after planting. Keep the soil damp, but not too wet, or else seeds will catch fungal infections and die. The best overhead cover is half shade using a single layer of babaçu or inajá leaves suspended about 2 m over the plantings. Once the seeds begin to germinate, the seedlings will sprout leaves quickly, standing 15–25 cm tall, with 4–8 simple leaves. They will rest for about a month before producing new leaves again—some of these will be compound leaves, and if the seedling is healthy, it can grow 10–15 cm during the second flush. The best time to plant seedlings into forest gaps or into agricultural clearings is after the second batch of leaves has sprouted. Prune off all but the highest four or five leaves to reduce heat and water stress when planting in bright sun. Dig a hole the exact size of the seedling bag with a posthole digger and slide the seedling soil core into this hole intact, making sure to re-establish soil contact between the seedling and the forest soil. It is also possible to plant mahogany seeds directly into gaps and agricultural clearings, especially in areas that have been cleared by burning, as the burned areas offer reduced root and above-ground competition. Keep seeds dry *after collecting them, because there is a tendency for molds and fungi to damage them without any sign of attack.*[*]

I plan to germinate and plant some mahogany this year and will report back on my success or failure.

Mango

Mango is really easy to start from seed. It's not great at staying true to type but it's well worth growing anyhow. I've enjoyed the fruit from seedling mangoes before. Sometimes they're a little stringy or taste a bit like turpentine, but they also can be grafted very easily.

I once planted a mango pit in a pot on the windowsill in my office back when I had a mind-numbing office job. A month later I came in after the weekend and BOOM! There was a little tree there with great big unfolding leaves. Seedlings grow really fast because there's a ton of energy saved inside of that big mango pit. The easy way to get mangoes to sprout is to trim hard outer part of the pit off and take the soft embryo part out of the inside and plant it. Some mangoes are "mono-embryonic", meaning they have a single embryo inside the pit while other mangoes are "poly-embryonic", meaning that there is more than one embryo inside the pit. I've heard the poly-embryonic varieties are more true to type. If you eat a really good mango and plant the pit, you'll know if it's

---
[*] https://cites.org/eng/node/43908

poly-embryonic when you see multiple shoots emerge from the ground. Let one of them grow and it will probably turn out like its mother. If it's mono-embryonic, you're on your own and you better learn how to graft in case it decides to make something weird. They will fruit from seed in about four to six years. Though the trees can grow 60 to 80 feet tall, they are very responsive to pruning and can even be kept hedge-sized if you're diligent.

If you want to spend less time waiting for fruit, grow some seedlings and graft scion wood from a mature tree onto them.

Mangoes are not normally grown from cuttings, though from rumors on the 'net some people have apparently rooted them from cuttings.

I tried air-layering my Grandpa's mango tree without luck and eventually gave up; however, I've also seen videos from India where gardeners are air-layering mangoes successfully. It may depend on the variety or it may just be that Indians have greener thumbs than I do. Maybe mangoes just don't like me.

My recommendation: grow seeds, then graft onto them. It's easy enough.

Melon

Save melon seeds from fully ripe melons, wash them well, dry and store in the fridge. Plant melons in spring a half to an inch deep after all danger of frost. I have smashed rotten cantaloupe in the garden and had the seeds grow a month later into happy vines which fruited for me. I've also gotten melons out of compost piles. They seem to like lots of compost.

Mesquite

I grew mesquite from seed by scarifying the seeds with a pair of nail clippers, then soaking and planting. As for other methods, New Mexico State University notes:

Mesquite are very difficult to grow from cuttings. Research reports on the internet indicate that it is not impossible, but a very low percentage of the cuttings successfully form roots and grow. Mesquite trees are more commonly propagated by seeds or by grafting a desirable variety onto a seedling rootstock. Clonal propagation is used to increase many ornamental plants because it is a quick way to produce exact replicates of the parent plant in those plants. The mesquite is one of many plants that do not easily reproduce in this manner.

If you still want to try to grow mesquite trees from cuttings, take the cuttings at various times of the year (softwood cuttings from new growth in the spring, semi-hardwood cuttings in mid-summer, and dormant cuttings in fall or winter). Treat the cuttings with strong concentrations of rooting hormones and follow directions in any of the many plant propagation books available in libraries or bookstores. The softwood and semi-hardwood cuttings must be protected from desiccating and will require a greenhouse or other means of maintaining humidity around the cuttings.

One report indicated that layering was more effective than propagation by cuttings. To propagate the mesquite in this manner, wound the stem then treat the wound with rooting hormone. While the wound is still fresh, bury the wounded portion of the stem in potting soil (the growing end remaining out of the soil) or wrap the wounded area with moist, fibrous sphagnum moss. Then wrap the moss containing the wounded stem with plastic. Seal the top and bottom of the plastic to keep the sphagnum moss moist. It may be helpful to cover this plastic with aluminum foil to keep the rooting area dark (benefits root formation) and to prevent overheating in our bright New Mexico sunlight. [*]

I think I'll stick with seeds.

Mint

Mint makes lots of runners that often root right in the ground. These can be cut and planted elsewhere, just keep them well-watered until established.

Moringa

To grow moringa, plant seeds in warm, well-drained soil. If it is cool outside, they will rot in the ground. When I started them

---

[*] https://aces.nmsu.edu/ces/yard/2007/042807.html

for my plant nursery, I had to get a head start on the season before the plant shows started, yet because of the chilly weather in late winter, they wouldn't grow unless I put the pots on a heat mat I set up on my back porch. If you have cool days and nights but want to start moringa in late winter/early spring, I suggest you use a greenhouse or use heating mats.

Like the seeds, moringa seedlings are also subject to rot, so make sure you don't overwater. The seedlings grow very very quickly and can actually start producing flowers and pods of their own within a year from planting. From seed, the moringa can hit 10' during its first year of growth. In the tropics the tree has reportedly reached 60' in height, yet I never see them much more than 30' or so, often less. My two-year-old moringa trees were over 20' tall. If you live in a northern climate you can plant seeds in spring and grow moringa as a green vegetable, harvesting and drying the leaves.

Moringa trees can also be propagated by sticking limbs in the ground; however, seedling trees are much stronger.

Morning Glory

Nick the seeds, then soak overnight and plant. Be sure to give them space to climb and know that some species will prolifically self seed. This is great in a corner of the yard, but not in your garden. Incidentally, the seeds of blue morning glories are hallucinogenic. I ate a few once and suffered no ill effects except for seeing a halo around the mailman's head when he delivered my mail that afternoon. Of course, the mailman may have simply been an angel. I find this unlikely, though the Priority Mail service can work almost supernaturally fast.

Mulberry

Mulberries are generally easy to start from cuttings, with two exceptions:

1. Don't try to start mulberry cuttings from trees while they're blooming or in fruit

I found this out from Michael at the Edible Plant Project. The strike rate is really poor because they'll try to fruit, rather than root. You'll have much better luck if you try later in the year.

2. Some Mulberry Species Root Easily—Some Don't

There are Pakistan long mulberry trees with beautiful long fruit—those are really hard to start from cuttings and need to be grafted instead. Red mulberries (*Morus rubra*) are tougher to root, as are black mulberries (*Morus nigra*). I've had white mulberries (*Morus alba*) root the easiest, but I've had luck with all three after enough attempts. Rooting mulberry cuttings isn't always possible... but you lose nothing by attempting.

Now let's get to it.

My method of rooting cuttings is moderately simple. I cut semi-hard wood twigs that are about 3/8" to 1/2" in diameter and 6–8" long. (That's new growth, but not so new it's soft and green.) Chopping a branch into multiple lengths will work. I then dip the bottom end into rooting hormone and poke a few of them at a time into small pots filled with potting soil or seed starting mix, then water well so the soil is damp. Then, I put clear plastic 1-gallon Ziploc bags over the tops of the pots to make mini-greenhouses, and rubber band them in place. This keeps the moisture in. If the leaves dry out, they're dead. These pots then sit in full shade until they root. Every few days, I'll pull the bags off (being careful not to disturb the cuttings) to let some air in and check to make sure the soil is still moist. After a few weeks, they'll start to root, and after about a month, you're probably good to take the bags off for good. Just keep misting them occasionally with the hose until they (hopefully) take. Some cuttings may not make it—and some will mold. Don't worry. Do a bunch and you're bound to get some strikes. All of them may take—and in that case, share the bounty with friends.

When the cuttings seem good and established, I turn the pots over and separate the well-rooted baby trees into pots of their own. At this point, I also put them into half-sun. They need to get acclimated to sunlight for a while. Full sun can burn the new growth.

For a better strike rate on mulberry cuttings, start them under intermittent mist like a nursery would do it.

Green Deane shares an even easier method in his post on mulberries at eattheweeds.com:

Mulberries, in my case, Morus rubra, *are full of life. One spring I trimmed my mulberry and used the branches for stakes. They sprouted. Not one to get in nature's way I dug them up, gave them to a friend, and they are still growing.*[*]

I've stuck some big 1" diameter sticks in the dirt in my backyard to see if they would do the same for me—and it didn't work.

Mustard

From seed, mustard germinates quickly and you can start harvesting leaves in about a month. Depending on the variety, you can get purple leaves... curly leaves... or even huge leaves. if you let the plant go to seed, after you save some seeds for next year, you can make your own delicious mustard with the rest.

Natal Plum (*Carissa macrocarpa*)

Julia F. Morton writes:

Seeds germinate in 2 weeks but the seedlings grow very slowly at first and are highly variable. Vegetative propagation is preferred and can be done easily by air-layering, ground-layering, or shield-budding. Cuttings root poorly unless the tip of a young branchlet is cut half-way through and left attached

---

[*] http://www.eattheweeds.com/mulberry-glucose-controlling-hallucinogen-2/

to the plant for 2 months. After removal and planting in sand, it will root in about 30 days. Grafting onto seedlings of the karanda (q.v.) has considerably increased fruit yield ... Seedlings may begin to produce fruit in 2 years; cuttings earlier.[*]

I rooted natal plum from semi-hardwood cuttings in the Taylor Gardens Nursery mist house. It took about two months for them to root. I have never tried them from seeds.

Noni

Spit fresh seeds into the soil and cover with an inch of soil. They'll emerge in a month or two. They are also easy to start from cuttings.

Noni can fruit from seeds or cuttings within a year.

Papaya

Papaya are easy to grow from seed. The easiest method I've seen is to scoop the seeds out of a fruit, goop and all, then plant them in a pot or in the ground. Multiple shoots will emerge in a month or so. When they sprout, select out the very best-looking ones, then chop the rest of them down with a pair of scissors. At a foot tall, aim to have them down to five or six per 3-gallon pot, then transplant them out into other pots or right in the ground.

---

[*] https://hort.purdue.edu/newcrop/morton/carissa.html

From seed, papaya can bloom in six months and bear fruit within a year.

Passionfruit

Julia F. Morton writes:

> *Passionfruit vines are usually grown from seeds. With the yellow form, seedling variation provides cross-pollination and helps overcome the problem of self-sterility. Some say that the fruits should be stored for a week or two to allow them to shrivel and become perfectly ripe before seeds are extracted. If planted soon after removal from the fruit, seeds will germinate in 2 to 3 weeks.*

> *Cleaned and stored seeds have a lower and slower rate of germination. Sprouting may be hastened by allowing the pulp to ferment for a few days before separating the seeds, or by chipping the seeds or rubbing them with fine sandpaper. Soaking, often recommended, has not proved helpful. Seeds are planted 1/2 in (1.25 cm) deep in beds, and seedlings may be transplanted when 10 in (25 cm) high. If taller—up to 3 ft (.9 in)—the tops should be cut back and the plants heavily watered.*

> *Some growers prefer layers or cuttings of matured wood with 3 to 4 nodes. Cuttings should be well rooted and ready for setting out in 90 days. Rooting may be hastened by hormone*

treatment. Grafting is an important means of perpetuating hybrids and reducing nematode damage and diseases by utilizing the resistant yellow passionfruit rootstock. If seeds are available in the early spring, seedlings for rootstocks can be raised 4 in (10 cm) apart in rows 24 in (60 cm) apart and the grafted plants will be ready to set out in late summer. If seeds cannot be obtained until late summer, the seedlings are raised and grafted in pots and set out in the spring. Scions from healthy young vines are preferred to those from mature plants. The diameter of the selected scion should match that of the rootstock. Either a cleft graft, whip graft, or side-wedge graft may be made.

If approach-grafting is to be done, a row of potted scions must be placed close alongside the row of rootstocks so that the union can be made at about 3/4 of the height of the plant.[*]

I have not propagated passionfruit myself, but my friend Garvin told me that he cleans the seeds right from fresh fruits and plants them and they germinate quickly.

Pawpaw (*Asimina spp.*)

Pawpaw seed germination requires a few steps. It's about a half-year process but it's not hard. It just takes time.

If your pawpaw seed dries out, your pawpaws will fail. If they're old seeds, they'll fail. Unless they've been taken from

---

[*] https://www.hort.purdue.edu/newcrop/morton/passionfruit.html

a ripe fruit and popped right into the refrigerator and kept slightly moist, the embryos will dry out and die. Pawpaws are not like beans! Get fresh seed!

Now you need to give your *Asimina triloba* seeds a good chilling in the refrigerator. This is called "stratifying" the seeds. Pop them in the fridge for four months in a baggie of slightly moist peat moss or potting soil. (I haven't germinated any species of pawpaw other than *A. triloba*, so you're on your own with *A. parviflora*, *A. pygmaea*, etc.)

Once you've had the seeds in the fridge for four months, plant them in spring. They will germinate a couple of months later in early summer.

Pawpaw can fruit from seed in 3–4 years.

Peaches and Nectarines

Some years ago I discovered in some dusty corner of the internet that peach pits require cold stratification to germinate.

I put this knowledge to the test with great success, starting about 50 peach pits I found beneath an abandoned and squirrel-ravaged Tropic Beauty peach growing a few miles from my old place in North Florida.

I did this despite the fact that there are hordes of small-minded gardeners in the world who take great pleasure in lecturing everyone about the utter worthlessness of starting fruit trees from seed.

These people are wrong. And boring. And stupid. And they smell.

In their second year, my two seedling peach trees produced about five gallons of fruit. They continued to massively outproduce the grafted peach trees I planted before them, plus they grew with more vigor.

Peaches are very easy to propagate via grafting and can be grafted onto plum, nectarine and apricot.

Pear

Germinate the same as apple.

Pecan

See walnuts.

Pepper

I cut open fully ripe pepper fruit, scrape out the seeds, then dry them on paper towels. Be careful with hot peppers, as saving seeds can get a little painful if you touch your eyes without thinking. Or scratch the inside of your nose. Once the seeds are dry, stick them in a sealed baggie or container and store in the fridge for the next growing season.

Plant pepper seeds a quarter to half-inch deep after all danger of frost and water as needed. Sweet peppers live less than a year when I grow them but hot peppers can perennialize in mild climates. My friend Eddy had a big three-year-old cayenne pepper bush that was around my height and loaded with peppers.

Perennial Cucumber / Ivy Gourd

The perennial cucumber (*Coccinea grandis*) is a small Indian cucumber with a bad reputation for being invasive. However, it is dioecious so if there isn't a male plant, none of the seeds on the female plants will be viable. Unscrupulous eBay sellers regularly sell seed from *C. grandis* which refuses to germinate, so don't fall into that trap. The best way to grow it is by dividing roots, busting off a sucker, or starting the vines from cuttings. They root easily in a mini-greenhouse or under mist. Just be careful— even without a male, the vines will root along the ground and become weedy if unmanaged.

Persimmon

Stratify for a few months, then plant in pots. Alternately, plant seeds directly in the ground in fall and let them come up when they wish in the spring. Persimmon cuttings do not root, but the tree can be grafted. American persimmons (*Diospyros virginiana*) are a common rootstock for the weaker-rooted Japanese persimmon (*Diospyros kaki*).

Pine

I have not germinated pine seeds, but Mother Earth News shares the following on growing pines from seed:

> To start growing pine trees from seed, gather large brown (or slightly green) cones in fall. The cones should be closed; if open,

they probably have already released their seeds. Toogood says trees that have a lot of cones are more likely to have viable seeds. Lay the cones in an open box at room temperature. When dry, the cones will open and release their seeds. If they don't open, place the box in a hot spot (104 to 113 degrees Fahrenheit) until they do. Use tweezers to remove any remaining seeds inside the cones.

To improve odds of germination, stratify the seeds: Mix them with moist peat or sand, place them in a clear plastic bag, and refrigerate them for three to seven weeks. (If the seeds germinate in the refrigerator, sow them immediately.) Sow the seeds in 3-inch pots, and provide bottom heat of about 60 degrees. Seedlings can be transplanted outdoors into larger pots in spring, when they're about 2 inches tall (six to eight weeks after they germinate).*

Pineapple

When I was a kid my grandpa had one of the workers at Publix supermarket save him all the pineapple tops she was cutting off when making fruit salad trays. She saved him a whole black trash bag full, then my grandpa paid my sisters and their friends a nickel apiece to plant the tops all through his backyard landscaping and around his trees. Within a couple of years, Grandpa was regularly harvesting fresh pineapples. He didn't

---

* https://www.motherearthnews.com/organic-gardening/growing-pine-trees-from-seed-zm0z13onzsor

water them, though I do think I remember him sending me out to fertilize them with some chemical fertilizer at one point. Even in lousy South Florida sand under off-and-on drought conditions, his pineapples produced.

The National Horticulture Board of India recommends the following procedures for propagating pineapple plants:

Pineapple is very easy to propagate vegetatively. Suckers arising in the axil of the leaves on the main stem form roots and can be used for propagation. Even the crown of leaves above the fruit and parts of the stem itself can be used. Another method of propagation is by slips, which are the suckers, arising immediately below the fruit. Suckers and slips should be preferred for planting as they come to bearing earlier than the crown and produce larger fruits. Before planting, suckers are sorted out into larger, medium and small to avoid competition between plants of different sizes. Too large suckers or slips should not be used for planting. Suckers weighing 400– 500 g or slips of 350–450 g are considered suitable as planting material. Prior to planting curing of slips and suckers for 8– 10 days in shade is necessary as fresh suckers planted in moist soil begin to decay. Before planting some of the lower leaves are removed from the sucker to facilitate the formation and entry of roots into the soil.

(http://nhb.gov.in/pdf/fruits/pineapple/pin011.pdf)

I have tried starting pineapples from seed without luck, so I just stick to breaking off slips and chopping off the tops of pineapples, then planting them here and there where I have space. It's a low-work backyard fruit.

Plum

Treat the same way as peaches, without removing the kernels from the pits.

Potato

Potatoes are usually propagated by cutting tubers into pieces with an eye or three each, then planting in the ground in early spring. However, potatoes can also be grown from seed. In her excellent book *Breed Your Own Vegetable Varieties* (pages 7–9), Carol Deppe shares the story of a potato breeder who started growing varieties as a hobby and now works with three hundred varieties:

> *Ewald Eliason, age seventy-three, is a retired Minnesota dairy farmer. He started breeding his own potatoes seventeen years ago. 'I've always enjoyed gardening,' he says, 'and potatoes are my favorite.'*
>
> *...*
>
> *[S]ince potatoes are propagated from tubers, not seed, all Ewald has to do to maintain a variety is plant its tubers. The*

resulting plants are clones of and genetically identical to the mother plant, whether insects are cross-pollinating the flowers or not.

Ewald started breeding potatoes just by saving true seed from the plants in his garden. The tuber pieces that are used as starts are called seed, so potato breeders say 'true seed' when they mean the product of sexual reproduction. Since potato cultivars are maintained by vegetative propagation, they are usually not genetically pure. When true seed is planted, the seedlings are individuals, each genetically different from its parents and all others. When such a plant forms tubers, it is an instant new variety.

Fertilized potato flowers form berries that resemble small green tomatoes. Each contains about two hundred seeds. Ewald picks the ripe berries, puts them in a food blender with water, and blends very briefly. The seeds sink, and the pulp floats. He plants the seeds in pots in a cold frame and transplants to his garden.

. . .

Ewald plants fifty to one hundred from each cross he does. Virtually all the plants from his various crosses give him hills of usable potatoes. Some plants don't yield well, however, and others are scabby. Most plants are pretty good, he finds, but not all are worth increasing and maintaining. During the growing season Ewald evaluates the potato plants—how vigorous they are, and how disease free. At the end of the season he digs the potatoes and looks at them. He likes potatoes that 'grow clean'—that are scab free and blight resistant. He also makes notes about the yield. Then, during the winter, he evaluates the potatoes for keeping and eating quality.

Ewald grows twelve 100-foot rows of potatoes per year, but since he has about three hundred varieties he doesn't usually have very much of any of them. His soil is sandy loam and he has subsurface water. He doesn't have to irrigate, even during droughts. He never sprays, either. He gardens organically. Presumably, he is selecting for varieties that perform well under organic gardening methods.

. . .

Ewald Eliason is still breeding more and more potatoes. 'When you grow all the various plants and dig them up, every one is a surprise,' he says. 'They're like children in a family. You just don't know what you're going to get.

I highly recommend you pick up a copy of Carol's book if you have any interest in vegetable breeding. She shares many inspiring stories like Ewald's, as well as a ton of information on the nitty gritty of plant breeding and seed-saving to create new varieties. If you have little fruits growing on your potato plants, why not try growing a few of the seeds and see what happens?

Pumpkins and Squash

Save seeds from fully ripe pumpkins and squash. The inner cavity of pumpkins and winter squashes is filled with a stringy mess of pumpkin bits and seeds. This isn't the "good eating" part of the pumpkin, so it's not worth trying to save any of the stringy mass, except for the seeds.

I dump the guts and seeds into a colander and swish them around under running water to clean them out, smashing the goop through the holes and separating the strings. If you'd like to save pumpkin seeds for eating rather than planting, you can just go directly to roasting them at this point.

For seed-saving purposes, I've sometimes let pumpkin guts sit on the counter for a few days and rot around the seeds. This smells bad but really loosens up the seeds when you wash them out. I think it may also increase the germination rate but I haven't tried a side-by-side trial.

Seed-covered paper towels on counters, window sills, shelves, tabletops, dressers and even the bathroom counter are common in our house during the fall as we save pumpkin seeds alongside the other heirlooms we want to plant in our spring gardens.

Spread your pumpkin seeds out someplace where they won't get wet again. Make sure they aren't too wet when you spread them out (sometimes I pat them down with one paper towel, then spread them onto a second) and have good air circulation as you most definitely do not want them germinating on your counter. They should dry fast. This will also keep them from molding as easily in storage and potentially losing their ability to germinate.

For summer squash, let the fruits ripen up on the plants until the stems turn brown, then harvest and save the seeds.

Radish

Radishes were my favorite vegetable to grow when I was a kid. I didn't really like eating them all that much, but they germinated in a few days and were ready in a month and that really suited my ADD style of gardening. SO FAST!

Radishes go to seed readily, with pretty little yellow flowers. Let them make pods and harvest the pods when they turn brown. Be careful, as the pods will shatter easily and spread the tiny red-brown seeds all over the place.

Rose

Roses grow readily from stem cuttings and air layering. My daughter starts them all the time using the mini-greenhouse method. Use 4–6" semi-hardwood cuttings and dip the ends in rooting hormone. Rooting usually takes a couple of months.

Rosemary

Rosemary starts easily from stem cuttings. Do not overwater, and use a well-draining medium.

As for seeds, West Coast Seeds recommends the following practice on their website:

Sow indoors mid-February to mid-April. Transplant or direct sow starting in late May, once soil has warmed. Starting indoors is more reliable. Use bottom heat to maintain an optimal soil temperature of 27–32°C (80–90°F).

… Germination is notoriously low, so plant more seeds than you plan to grow on. Sow them barely covered with steril- ized seed starting mix over bottom heat. Once germinated, rosemary is highly prone to damping off, so keep watering to a minimum, provide bright light, and ventilation. Keep each plant in its own pot for the first winter and offer them protection from severe cold. Transplant to the garden the following spring at a spacing of 60–90 cm (24–36").[*]

Ah, so that's why everyone starts them from cuttings.

Sapodilla

Sapodilla grows easily from seed and will fruit in 5–8 years. Julia Morton recommends veneer grafting to ensure good fruit varieties and faster production and also notes that air layering and cuttings do not work.

---

[*] https://www.westcoastseeds.com/blogs/how-to-grow/grow-rosemary

Sea Beans and Drift Seeds

There are quite a wide variety of "sea beans" and drift seeds that wash up on beaches after being carried hundreds or even thousands of miles by the tides. I love these adventurous plants and have germinated multiple different types over the years.

For sea hearts, donkey eyes and hamburger beans, saw a notch in the bean with a pocket knife or file, soak it in water until it swells up, then plant. Piercing the seed coat takes patience as they are very hard—don't cut yourself!

When I nicked and soaked a hamburger bean (*Mucuna urens*), it germinated in a little over a week. It grew about 12" in a couple of days and started rotating around in a circle looking for something to grasp. It moved so fast that my wife and I sat on the porch and watched it make an entire rotation in about an hour. I stuck a little pole in for it to grab, which it did—and twisted itself completely tight to it within another hour's time. It lived for two years in my North Florida garden, freezing down and coming back after the first winter, then dying in the second without producing any blooms.

The big sea heart (*Entada gigas*), also known as the monkey ladder vine, thrives in Costa Rica and is the seed of a gigantic jungle liana that makes the largest legume pod. If you get one to grow, chances are you won't be able to grow it unless you live in the jungle where it can scramble up the side of a giant tree. Try anyway, though! It would be awesome to see in a backyard.

Another crazy seed you may find on beaches, especially in Asia, is the pod of the fish poison tree, aka *Barringtonia asiatica*. This is a large, boxy fruit about half the size of a coconut. Carefully slit the husk down the sides and crack it away in slices to get to the pit in the interior, then plant in well-drained soil. The trees are really beautiful and attract bats and moths at night with their sweet-scented flowers.

Mangrove propagules are another adventurous "seed" you'll find on beaches. Plant them rounded side down in a cup of muck and they'll root and grow, putting up a shoot with beautiful, leathery leaves. I've started them in jars and in ponds.

Soapnut / Soapberry

I have heard that soap nut trees (*Sapindus saponaria*) take 8 years or longer to produce fruit when grown from seed, however my friend Alex Ojeda of Permaculture Jax told me that his soapberry trees bore fruit only three years after germination. I'll take his first-hand account over anything on the internet.

Germination is easy with soapberry trees. I scarified a bunch of seeds and planted them in little pots for my plant nursery and got almost a 100% germination rate.

Like many uncommonly cultivated species, the soapberry needs a mate for pollination. Trees come in male, female and hermaphroditic varieties. Only females and hermaphrodites will bear soap nuts. If you plant three, chances are really good that at least one or two of them will fruit for you.

I planted five in my old food forest, because really... won't the Econopocalypse be better when you can take a nice shower between bouts of killing diseased and drug-crazed looters with a broken shovel?

Soapberry trees grow tall with an airy, open habit. In fact, they look a lot like the despised Chinaberry tree that's invaded railroad tracks and roadsides across the state, though unlike Chinaberry they have almost white bark. They're quite attractive.

If you have a small yard, I recommend planting three in a tight triangle so they grow like a triple-trunked tree and will pollinate each other without taking up too much space. That's what I did in my backyard, spacing them about 6' apart, though you could probably plant three in the same hole about 18" apart and it would look really cool.

Starfruit

Starfruit propagation is similar to its cousin bilimbi. They start readily from seed and can also be grafted.

Stinking Toe

Stinking toe, also known more pleasantly as the West Indian locust, is a large leguminous tree which bears large pods filled with what tastes like a sweet Graham-cracker flour. They are highly nutritious and pleasant to eat, though some people think they have a bad smell. They don't have any negative aroma that I can pick up, but I may be genetically deficient in some way, as I also don't mind the smell of noni fruit, cigars, Limburger, or gasoline.

Strawberry

I have read about growing strawberries from seed but haven't attempted it. One of my children did, but the seeds failed to germinate. It's easy to just take pups from existing plants and pot them up or plant them out. Keep the new plants watered decently and they'll grow quickly. Pro-tip: strawberries love fish emulsion fertilizer.

Sugar Apple

Sugar apple grows readily from seed, usually germinating in a few weeks. Julia F. Morton writes more on propagation in her book *Fruits of Warm Climates*:

> *Sugar apple seeds have a relatively long life, having kept well for 3 to 4 years. They germinate better a week after removal from the fruit than when perfectly fresh. Germination may take 30 days or more but can be hastened by soaking for 3 days or by scarifying. The percentage of germination is said to be better in unsoaked seeds. While the tree is generally grown from seed, vegetative propagation is practiced where the crop is important and early fruiting is a distinct advantage.*

Seedlings may be budded or grafted when one-year old. In India, selected clones grafted on A. reticulata *seedlings have flowered within 4 months and fruited in 8 months after planting out, compared with 2 to 4 years in seedlings. The grafted trees are vigorous, the fruits less seedy and more uniform in size.* A. senegalensis *is employed as a rootstock in Egypt.* A. glabra *is suitable but less hardy. The sugar apple itself ranks next after* A. reticulata *as a rootstock. In India, budding is best done in January, March and June. Results are poor if done in July, August, November or December unless the scions are defoliated and debudded in advance and cut only after the petioles have dehisced. Side-grafting can be done only from December to May, requires much skill and the rate of success has not exceeded 58.33%. Shield-budding gives 75% success and is the only commercially feasible method.*

Inarching is 100% successful. Cuttings, layers, airlayers have a low rate of success, and trees grown by these techniques have shallow root systems and cannot endure drought as well as seedlings do.

Despite most methods of propagation not working on sugar apple, its ability to fruit rapidly from seed is a plus.

Sugarcane

All you need is a good hunk of sugarcane with a couple of intact nodes (those are the joints in the cane). Since sugarcane is usually harvested in the fall, that's the time you're likely to see the canes for sale. Cut canes into segments with at least 3–4 nodes each, pick a good spot to plant them, then put those pieces on their sides about 4–6" down and cover them up well.

When I plant sugarcane in November, the plants always pop up for me sometime in March or April. For each cane you bury, you'll usually get a couple of good shoots emerging from the ground.

You can also propagate by dividing clumps of existing cane.

In the tropics, you can plant any time and they will grow quickly, though it's probably best to time your plantings with the advent of the rainy season.

Sweet Potato

Have you ever stuck a few toothpicks into a sweet potato from the store, stuck it in a glass, filled the glass with water, then watched it grow lush and abundant vines?

If not, grab a sweet potato and try it. The new vines that form can be broken off and planted in the ground once they get to be a few inches long. The potato will continue producing new ones for months. These little vines are called "slips".

You can also bury sweet potatoes on their sides in a pot or flat of soil and use the vines as they emerge.

Make sure to keep them watered as they get established. Once they're established, they'll grow like weeds. You can cut chunks of vine from established plantings and use them to start

Rooting a sweet potato in water

new beds. Just cut off pieces of vines and plant them. The vines you plant don't need to have any roots. Just stick and water decently for a week or two until they start growing.

Tamarind

Tamarind have very hard seeds. For good germination rates without the wait, scarify, soak overnight, then plant. They'll come up in a few weeks. You can also graft tamarind and grow them from air layers as well as semi and soft-wood cuttings. Seedling trees may take six or more years to fruit. This is likely to be shortened by vegetatively propagating them or grafting.

Tobacco

Because of their minute size, tobacco seeds need to be planted differently than most other seeds. To add an extra layer of fun, they also need light for germination—and when they do germinate, the seedlings are really, really tiny. This is why it's really difficult to direct-seed tobacco in your garden. Chances are, the sun will wipe your plants out before they develop into anything—even if you have a totally perfect little square foot bed—so instead of planting them right in the soil, it makes sense to start them in carefully managed flats. These flats can be made from just about anything. I used to use egg cartons but I found that the soil in them dried out too quickly so I switched to using home-made wooden flats that are about 4" deep.

To plant tobacco, prepare a fine soil surface in your flat or container, make sure it's good and damp, and then simply sprinkle the tiny seeds across it. Mist your seeds with your spray bottle, and make sure the flats are in the shade—if they're not, you may dry out the soil and kill the plants before they emerge. If you live in an arid climate, you might want to cover your flats with some plastic wrap to keep in moisture. To avoid mold problems, I'd take the plastic off once a day and mist the ground when I did. If you don't cover with plastic, try and remember to mist your flats about twice a day or anytime you think of it. If they do dry out a bit, don't freak out. Moisten them well and keep your fingers crossed. I've had tobacco pull through even when I've been less than religious about my watering. Just do your best. In about 10–14 days, you should see tiny seedlings begin to emerge from the soil. They're so small you almost need a magnifying glass to see them at first.

Within a week or two, they'll get bigger—and in a month or so, they'll likely be an inch or so in height. As the seedlings grow, I thin out the flat with a pair of scissors, decapitating unwanted plants rather than pulling them out and disturbing the roots of their neighbors. Give each little plant its own space and their growth rate will be much higher.

When your plants get about 2–3" tall, transplant them to a second flat until they're large enough to transplant—or, if your weather is mild and the sun isn't too brutal, put them directly out into the garden. I usually wait until they hit about 6" before placing them in the garden, but I've had good luck with smaller plants as well. Tobacco grows quickly after transplanting. In a few months, they will bloom and the blooms quickly develop into small pods the size of olives. When these pods dry, they are ready to be harvested for seed. Inside each pod are thousands of tiny tobacco seeds, just like brown dust, waiting for you to plant them and start the cycle over again.

Tomato

Tomatoes can be grown from seeds and cuttings. You can also graft them onto potato plants, but that strikes me as the sort of thing witches used to get burned for. My wife prunes our tomato plants and sticks the cuttings in the ground and keeps them watered until they grow. I have also smashed a rotten tomato over a garden bed and raked it into the soil, then had tomatoes come up. They aren't picky. You'll read about proper seed saving techniques with letting the tomato pulp ferment, then taking the seeds from that, which is great if you want to put your seeds in storage until next season; however, I have also heard about a ring of tomato sprouts emerging from the ground where someone dropped a beefsteak tomato slice out of their Big Mac. I just dry seeds on paper towels, then stick the whole paper towel, complete with seeds glued to it, into a baggie and save for spring. In spring, I either pick the seeds off or plant chunks of paper towel right along with the seeds.

I know. It's crazy. But it works.

Turmeric

Plant turmeric in a spot with rich soil and mulch and you'll have it for years to come.

In the fall, winter and spring you can plant roots around your yard. I did this in my old North Florida food forest, just sticking turmeric roots in the ground here and there around my fruit trees.

They won't emerge until right around the beginning of summer and will sleep happily beneath the earth until then. You can plant turmeric anywhere from 2–6" deep and it still comes up. I go for about 4" down. They'll grow in shade and sun.

Don't be anxious in the spring for your turmeric to show up. It won't. You'll think it's dead, you'll be sad, you'll doubt your gardening ability, you'll give up on your faith…

…and then, sometime in June, little shoots will emerge and you'll repent of your doubt.

Growing turmeric is a great idea for multiple reasons. It's an anti-cancer herb, it's easy to grow, it's high-value and it's a wonderful culinary spice. It's also pretty in an edible landscaping plan. Just know that it sleeps half the year.

Mine dies down in November and comes back year after year in a bigger clump.

Make sure your turmeric aren't getting too much water during their winter dormancy. Though it hasn't happened to me yet, I've heard that can induce rot and kill your plants. Wet summers and dry winters are perfect for growing happy turmeric.

Which leads me to the one downside of growing turmeric: it takes two years for a good clump.

You may grow it faster in the tropics but in zone 8/9 where I used to grow it I couldn't get a good yield until two years after planting. I harvest when the tops die back in fall. Fortunately, it's so easy to grow and takes up so little space that you can pretty much plant turmeric and forget about it.

When you pull up the roots, wash them, let them dry a little, then store in the crisper drawer. They'll also keep on the counter for a few weeks but are subject to drying out.

Note: If you live north of zone 8, turmeric also grows EAS-ILY as a potted plant. Just bring it in during the winter and don't give it too much water. After two years, dump out the pot and voila—roots! Plant them and make more!

Vanilla Orchid

Vanilla orchids are propagated via stem cuttings. Cut a foot or two of vine off a plant, being careful not to break the tender stems. Then bury the bottom half of the cutting in mulch next to a tree and let the vine start climbing. Vanilla apparently does not like being properly planted in soil, preferring to root into mulch. I got mine to start by just laying the cutting on the ground next to a small tree and throwing some rotting yard waste over the bottom of the stem. They rooted and grew well.

Walnut

I only germinated walnuts once. I got them in one of those assortments of nuts you get around the holidays at the grocery store. I buried them in the ground in fall and waited until spring, when they sprouted. According to Richard Jauron at Iowa State University, I did the right thing:

Collect walnuts after they fall to the ground. Remove the husks and then place the nuts in water. Nuts that float are not viable and can be discarded. Good, viable nuts will sink to the bottom.

Before the walnuts will germinate, the nuts need to be exposed to cold temperatures and moist conditions. The cold-moist requirement can be met by planting the nuts in the ground in fall. Plant walnuts 1 to 2 inches deep.

The cold-moist requirement can also be accomplished through a process called stratification. Walnuts can be stratified by placing the nuts in a moist mixture of sand and peat moss and then storing them in a cool location. Suitable containers include coffee cans, plastic buckets, and food storage bags. The refrigerator is a good storage location. (Stratification temperatures should be just above freezing.) The walnuts must remain in the refrigerator for 90 to 120 days. After the nuts have been *properly stratified, they can be removed from the refrigerator and planted.*[*]

Plant in the ground if you're feeling lucky—stick them in the fridge and keep an eye on them if you need control!

Pecans grow the same way.

Yams (*Dioscorea spp.*)

My experiment with growing yams from cuttings was like this: I just took a few little cuttings with a couple of nodes each, then put them in pots and stuck them in a mist house that a friend with a nursery owned. A month or so later, I had rooted yams ready for planting.

Many yam species have aerial "bulbils" (roots) that you can plant for the next year's harvest. Some do not.

Yams are only rarely grown from seeds except for breeding purposes—and if you live in the US, you're unlikely to have a long enough warm season or proper light cycles for them to even bloom.

The normal method of propagation is via bulbils for the varieties that produce bulbils, and via divided roots for those that do not.

---

[*] https://hortnews.extension.iastate.edu/2008/8-27/walnuts.html

If you don't have bulbils, you need to make "minisetts". All that requires is a good yam root, a knife, and perhaps some ashes to ward off potential soil pests.

This is the minisett method of yam propagation. If you have bulbils, you can just use those; however, some yam species don't make bulbils, or you may be starting with a store-bought yam and don't want to plant the whole thing. A good-sized yam can get you a dozen or more plants if you divide it well.

To propagate yams from minisetts, get a fresh yam and cut it into pieces while ensuring you have a good piece of skin on each one from which the new growth will emerge.

You can cut the yam pieces even smaller than I cut them in the video. Half that size will still work. Larger pieces will give you stronger vines, however, so there's a balance between getting more plants and getting more vigorous plants.

Dip the cut pieces of yam in ashes and let them dry a bit.

Ashes seem to help heal the wound and protect it from infection. It's a traditional method practiced in places where yams are grown. Pieces will also grow without ashes, but it's an easy step so I follow it.

It's important to plant yams in loose soil as they are a root crop.

In Florida sand I just dug a little hold and buried them and they'd get nice and big; however, in clay it's important to loosen lots of space to give the roots a place to grow.

If you like, you can plant your yam minisetts in a big pot or a bed to ensure you only get ones that will sprout. When the vines start popping out from the ground, transfer your yams to where you would like them to grow—and don't wait long—the vines will grow fast and become a big tangle if you don't act quickly.

Ensure each yam has a solid stick they can climb. Shoot for 6–7' tall poles or ever larger.

Yam bulbils will also work for planting if you have access to them; however, not all *Dioscorea* species will make bulbils.

Note: I have successfully propagated *Dioscorea alata* from cuttings, but I don't think that method will give you good yields, at least in the first year. If you can't get roots or bulbils, go for it, though.

Usually it's just easier to propagate yams by cutting big roots up into minisetts. Try your local ethnic market for yams and other treasures.

With the potato yam (*Dioscorea esculenta*), just use entire roots from the cluster without cutting them into pieces, as that is supposed to work better.

The potato yam grows a cluster of roots around a small, central "head" from which the main vine emerges. Each of these roots can be cut off and planted to create a new cluster of roots.

Zinnia

Zinnias were the first flower I ever grew and are wonderfully easy to grow as well as being. As my Uncle Stuart put it, "Zinnias are an encouraging flower." If you want to save zinnia seeds, wait until the flower heads dry out on the plant, then pull off the petals. At the base of almost every petal is a seed that looks like a spear point. Plant zinnia seeds about a quarter-inch deep after danger of frost. They usually germinate in 5–7 days.

No. I'm not going to talk about the 'Z' vegetable. It's not edible and you shouldn't grow it.

8

Conclusion

The methods I described in this book should give you the toolkit you need to propagate just about anything. Over time and with added experience, it gets easier and easier to propagate plants. Just the "nick and soak" method of seed germination opens up a huge range of possibilities. When you add in grafting, air layering, mist houses and all the other good stuff in this book, you'll be able to propagate just about any plant under the sun.

The biggest obstacle to success in propagation is our fear of failure. My 11-year-old son spent a few days this last week trying to build a pair of wings that would let him fly down the driveway. In his mind, it was worth trying and he swears he managed to get some lift from his tied-on wings made from broomsticks, bamboo strips and plastic sheeting.

I wish all of us would be so creative. To test and try and experiment without simply giving up as soon as someone says something isn't possible or is "too hard". That creative drive of a child seems to melt away as we get older. We don't want to try because we are afraid of failure. Quit thinking that way! Of course you'll fail! I have shared many of my propagation successes in this book, yet just ten feet from me by a window is a pot of rotten mulberry cuttings from a variety I really, really wanted to grow. It happens, but more often than not, you'll find success. It's the fear of trying that holds us back more than the actual failures. Better to try and fail than not to try at all. As I watched videos on YouTube of gardeners in India using muck and plastic bags to root air layers, I was struck by how complicated we've made things for ourselves. Do you need rooting hormone, disinfectant, a sharp knife and sphagnum moss with rubber hands to perform a successful air layer? Nope, no more than you need a BMW to get you across town. It may be nice and it might break down less than a beater, but it's not necessary. If life gives you a battered Corolla, drive it. If life takes your battered Corolla, ride a bike. Catch a bus. Hitchhike. It's better to keep moving, and if you keep moving in your propagation experiments, you'll have success after success.

If you have gardening questions, success stories or just want to send pictures of yourself in pink flip flops, my email address is david@floridafoodforests.com. Write any time—and until we meet again, may your thumbs always be green.

About the Author

David The Good is the author of eight gardening books, including *Totally Crazy Easy Florida Gardening*, *Grow or Die: The Good Guide to Survival Gardening*, *Compost Everything: The Good Guide to Extreme Composting*, and *The Easy Way to Start a Home-Based Plant Nursery and Make Thousands in Your Spare Time*. He's also the author of *Turned Earth: A Jack Broccoli Novel*, the world's first gardening thriller. David has written for *Mother Earth News*, *Permaculture Magazine*, *Backwoods Home*, *Heirloom Gardener Magazine*, *Stupefying Stories*, and *The Grow Network*, along with maintaining a popular YouTube channel. He and his wife Rachel currently live on a jungle homestead near the equator along with their eight children. In his spare time, David enjoys woodworking, oil painting, and building musical instruments. You can find him online at www.thesurvivalgardener.com.

CASTALIA HOUSE

NON-FICTION
Ship of Fools by C. R. Hallpike
Clio and Me by Martin van Creveld
Equality: The Impossible Quest by Martin van Creveld
Between Light and Shadow by Marc Aramini
Innocence & Intellect, 2001—2005 by Vox Day
Crisis & Conceit, 2006—2009 by Vox Day
Cuckservative by John Red Eagle and Vox Day
SJWs Always Lie by Vox Day
SJWs Always Double Down by Vox Day
Jordanetics by Vox Day
The Last Closet by Moira Greyland

FICTION
An Equation of Almost Infinite Complexity by J. Mulrooney
The Missionaries by Owen Stanley
The Promethean by Owen Stanley
Brings the Lightning by Peter Grant

SCIENCE FICTION
Soda Pop Soldier by Nick Cole
Pop Kult Warlord by Nick Cole
CTRL-ALT REVOLT! by Nick Cole
Superluminary by John C. Wright

FANTASY
The Green Knight's Squire by John C. Wright
Iron Chamber of Memory by John C. Wright
Awake in the Night by John C. Wright
Summa Elvetica by Vox Day
A Throne of Bones by Vox Day
A Sea of Skulls by Vox Day

CPSIA information can be obtained
at www.ICGtesting.com
Printed in the USA
LVHW041111280220
648389LV00001B/12